ADVANCE PRAISE FOR "FUTUREPROOF YOUR CAREER AND COMPANY"

"During his time with TTEC, Maulik lived our values to bring humanity and technology together for amazing customer and employee experiences. This book builds on that to examine what a future-proof business and leader looks like. A great read!"

Ken Tuchman, Chairman and CEO, TTEC

"Data. Technology. Virus. Change. Forces at work today so profound and vast, as to devastate known business models, and create new ones, overnight. Businesses operate in a Darwinian landscape - it will not be the biggest or the smartest which will survive, but those who adapt best to change. This is an insightful book crafted by a practitioner. It is practical, helpful, powerful."

Manny Pangilinan, Chairman and CEO, PLDT

"A great read that is well researched and full of laser guided quotes that bring the concepts to life. Maulik presents a sure-fire road map for starting a business or transforming a company that has lost its way."

Brian Delaney, President, Alorica Latin America and the Caribbean Operations

"This book has everything I look for: sharp analysis, humor and warmth, straightforward writing, compelling insight and a remarkable blend of theory and practice. The book provides crucial, actionable guidance for professionals who want to flourish."

Linda Green-Kiely, Entrepreneur and Co-founder, Voxpro

"As CEO of SPi Global, Maulik showed us the tremendous possibilities which comes from believing in your people. In this book, he shares insights on ways technology will impact business, and how building the right culture can ensure sustainable rewards for all stakeholders in the days ahead."

Brian Hong, Former Chairman, SPi Global

"What makes this future-proofing guidance even more powerful and exuberant is Maulik's experience backed by insights and moreover, his humanity and compassion to all people. A torch to guide you through the era of New Norm."

Takashi Amino, President and CEO, Relia, Inc.

"Eloquent and entertaining. Maulik effortlessly weaves relevant anecdotes and stories with actionable tips and insights. I highly recommend it."

Sigit Prasetya, Managing Partner and Head of Asia, CVC Capital Partners

"In this era of uncertainty coupled with the information and opinion overload, Maulik provides insightful hacks to deal with the exciting yet scary future with immense clarity and conviction. With his unique gripping and precise style, this book is hard to put down especially once you read the wonderful anecdotes opening each chapter. Don't miss."

Puneet Shivam, President, Avendus Capital US and Global Co-head, Enterprise Tech Services

"This gift box contains 10 perspectives to crystallize the shape of Future and 10 proposals to make it even brighter. Clear and convincing words brewed from Maulik's real experiences. A book to always keep at your side."

Shinya Imai, Chairman, Inspiro Relia Inc.

"I wear two hats - a leader to many at work and mom to three Gen Zers at home. This book resonated with me for both of these roles. I found it inspiring and informative."

Kylie Luo, Executive Director, BDO LLP, Singapore

"This book is relevant for every corner of this global village we live in. Leading a company in Japan, I found it helpful and insightful for the challenges I face over the next decade. I highly recommend it!"

Toru Izuta, CEO, JF Gourmet Card Company Ltd.

"For anyone on a journey to building a sustainable career and company in this rapidly changing world, this book offers both inspiration and insights. A must read."

Ray Espinosa, President and CEO, Meralco

"Maulik's timing is impeccable – while we are in the midst of an unprecedented crisis, right now most of us are looking for direction and guidance on how to futureproof our career / company. Whether you are a Gen Z about to join the workforce or a Baby Boomer at the peak of your career, whether you are employed, self-employed or unemployed, this powerful manifesto is the shake-up you need to get moving to claim the future."

Sanjiv Vohra, President and CEO, Security Bank

"Baseball philosopher Yogi Berra says "'It's tough to make predictions, especially about the future.'" But here comes a book that shows the reality of the future unfolding right before our eyes. Maulik makes the book so enjoyable to read. It is one of the rare gems that comes along as you would smile, laugh, contemplate, arrive at many "Aha moments!" that will educate and prepare us to explore and exploit the future. Love this book. I will recommend this to many."

Francis Kong, Entrepreneur, Columnist, Speaker, and Book Author

"Contact Center Industry is going through massive disruption thanks to digital revolution, artificial intelligence and the generational shift. This book is a must-read for anyone wanting to be the disruptor and not be disrupted."

Benedict Hernandez, Chairman, Contact Center Association of the Philippines

"Love Maulik's book, it almost reads like a template that can give you a map on how we can navigate through these challenging times. Couldn't be more timely, as we've seen how many companies have literally have had to Evolve or Die!"

Simon Calasanz, Former President, RCBC Bankard

"It's not just a book but a roadmap for leaders for how to traverse through the treacherous terrain ahead."

Roger Kidwell, COO, Netspend

"Organizations that invest time, effort and energy in futureproofing will annihilate those who don't. This book is a timely reminder. A must-read."

Dr. Apoorva Ranjan Sharma, Co-Founder and Managing Director, 9Unicorns Fund

"This book encourages one to not fear the fourth industrial revolution and be a catalyst for change to create value not just for oneself, but for businesses and communities as well."

Robin Heng, Global Market Head, Bank of Singapore

"How future-ready are we? The rise of technology has transformed the way we work and play. Maulik makes a convincing case on how we can future proof our companies and our careers today. A timely and inspirational read."

August Hatecke, Country Head Singapore, UBS AG

FUTUREPROOF *Your* CAREER & COMPANY

FUTUREPROOF *Your* CAREER & COMPANY

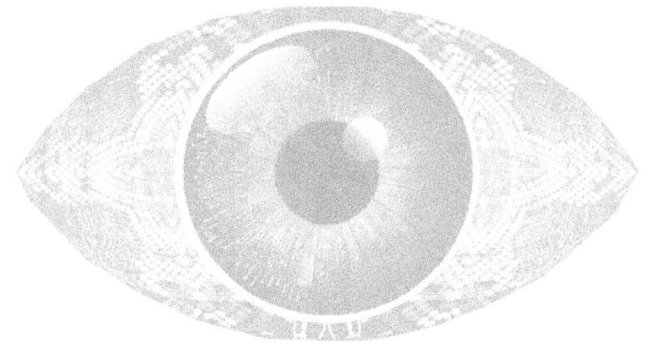

FLOURISH IN AN ERA OF
AI, DIGITAL NATIVES, & THE GIG ECONOMY

MAULIK PAREKH

Copyright © 2020 Maulik Parekh All Rights Reserved.

Published by Maulik Parekh.

ISBN: 9798561255632

No part of this publication may be reproduced, distributed, or transmitted in any form or by any means, including photocopying, recording, or other electronic or mechanical methods, without the prior written permission of the publisher, except in the case of brief quotations embodied in reviews and certain other non-commercial uses permitted by copyright law.

To my parents,

Ramniklal M. Parekh

Bhagirathi R. Parekh

DOWNLOAD A FREE FRAMEWORK

As a thank you for purchasing this book,
I'd like to offer you a FREE two-page framework
that summarizes the key takeaways from the book.
You may print it and keep it close to you for easy reference.

Please download the free framework here:
https://framework.futureproofyourcareerandcompany.com/

TABLE OF CONTENTS

Introduction 17

SECTION I THREE DISRUPTIVE FORCES 25
Chapter 1: Artificial Intelligence..27
Chapter 2: Digital Natives..41
Chapter 3: The Gig Economy..53

SECTION II FUTUREPROOF YOUR CAREER 67
Chapter 4: The Future is AI: Be a Human..69
Chapter 5: The Future is Change: Be a Catalyst...............................81
Chapter 6: The Future is People: Be an Alchemist 95
Chapter 7: The Future is Turbulent: Be a Captain 109
Chapter 8: The Future is Unknown: Be a Futurist.......................125

SECTION III FUTUREPROOF YOUR COMPANY 139
Chapter 9: The Future is Digital: Transform Business 141
Chapter 10: The Future is Meaningful: Infuse Purpose 153
Chapter 11: The Future is Boundless: Unleash Innovation 167
Chapter 12: The Future is New: Inspire Learning........................181
Chapter 13: The Future is Fun: Enjoy Expedition 195

The Future: Growth or Extinction 213

Thank You..219
Acknowledgments...221
Index..225
Notes..235

INTRODUCTION

> *"The measure of intelligence is the ability to change."*
> Albert Einstein

What do Alaska's pink salmon and Florida's green lizards have in common?

It's not an obscure riddle.

These creatures are rapidly evolving to thrive amidst the massive disruptions in their ever-changing environments.

Scientists are fascinated by the sheer speed of their evolution. It's not taking them thousands of years to change and adapt, but just a few years.

In Alaska, as the temperature of stream water rises with climate change, the pink salmon in Auke Creek migrate from the ocean to the river about two weeks earlier than they did just 40 years ago.[1]

The genetic changes needed to drive this behavior change evolved quickly, over just one or two generations. The salmon population that didn't genetically evolve and continued to arrive late has all but disappeared.

Meanwhile, Florida's green lizards were happily living perched on the trunks and lower branches of the trees.[2]

Life was good until their aggressive and invasive cousins — the brown lizards from Cuba and Bahama — arrived and claimed the same habitat as their own.

As a result of this unwelcome invasion, the green lizards started to move their homes up the trees. This was a big challenge as they needed a better grip to hold on to the smoother and thinner branches among the treetops.

Within fifteen years, the green lizards developed larger toepads and stickier toes. That meant a more reliable and secure grip in their new habitat. More importantly, it meant surviving and thriving in this new environment.

There are no IQ tests for salmon or lizards.

But based on how fast they are changing, it's safe to say Einstein would be impressed.

If Einstein was alive today, though, there is one thing that would make him scratch his hairy head. He would be unimpressed by how slowly some companies are changing, adapting, and evolving. And how quickly they are becoming extinct.

In the last ten years alone, we have witnessed mighty giants — niche leaders in their industries — such as Kodak, Blackberry, Toys R US, become all but extinct.

While they each have a unique and nuanced story about how they went from being a household name to extinction, there is a common thread across these three examples.

They chose not to swim upstream early. They chose not to climb the tree. They chose not to be resilient. They chose not to evolve, adapt, and change to the new paradigm, new environment, new competition.

Despite being the first company to invent the digital camera in 1975, Kodak failed to see digital photography as a disruptive technology.

Blackberry, named the fastest-growing company in the world by Fortune magazine in 2009, failed to realize that consumers want their smartphones to go beyond being mere communication devices. They want mobile entertainment portals.

Toys R US, once a market leader with enviable brand recognition, failed to realize the importance of having an online presence (literally giving their digital business to Amazon).

These companies are not alone.

According to Innosight, based on almost a century's worth of market data, companies in the S&P 500 list in 1964 stayed in the index for an average of 33 years. That number fell to 24 years in 2016 and is forecasted to fall to 12 years in 2027.[3]

The disruption is accelerating. Only the most agile will thrive.

Why write this book?

For two reasons. A professional and a personal reason.

For the past ten years, as a CEO of global companies with over 10,000 employees, I witnessed three powerful trends emerging and gaining momentum:

1. artificial intelligence tiptoeing into our workflows, our processes, and our jobs.
2. the digital generations starting to storm and transform the workplace.

3. the increasing popularity of freelancing changing not only who got the job done but also where, when, and how.

At first glance, these trends appear to be unrelated. After all, what could smart machines, younger generations, and the gig economy possibly have in common?

Digital revolution.

The exponential growth in computing power, data, and connectivity has nourished and nurtured these seemingly disparate forces.

Ironically, these trends are not only the *product* of this technological progress but also the *consumers*.

The more they consume, the faster, better, and smarter the technology evolves. The faster, better, and smarter the technology evolves, the more they consume.

This symbiotic and synergetic feeding frenzy is expected to peak over the next decade.

A weather forecast for the future?

A perfect storm.

As a part of my job, I was curious to know how leaders could navigate their teams, departments, and companies through this turbulence brewing on the horizon.

But in 2016, this professional curiosity became deeply personal. My first daughter, Clara, was born.

Overnight, the future became more meaningful.

More meaningful than churning out strategic roadmaps, expansion plans, and growth forecasts.

I found myself pondering what kind of world Clara would inherit, paying attention to every clue that gave me a glimpse into the future she will grow into, and wondering what skills she would need to succeed in the 21st Century.

The book is a product of this personal and professional curiosity.

A bit about the book

There are many books written by chest-thumping CEOs with a predictable plot — "Look what we have achieved. Follow the model, and you will succeed." If that's what you are looking for, you will be disappointed.

This book is the exact opposite.

The following pages are anchored in humility.

Why?

Because the future punishes the hubris of "know-it-all" but rewards the humility of "learn-it-all."

Humility to accept the fact that...what made us successful during the last decade may not make us successful during the next...we must evolve, adapt, and change...we must learn to unlearn and relearn.

The book is not pedantic. The words, sentences, and paragraphs are not complex nor long. If you are craving for complex and long, you will be disappointed.

The book is meant to be conversational — an easy read.

It's not meant to impress.

It's meant to inspire.

How to read this book?

The book is divided into three sections.

Section I dives deep into each trend: Artificial Intelligence, Digital Generations, and the Gig Economy. It covers...

- How powerful are these trends?
- Why should you pay attention to them?
- How will they impact your career and the company over the next decade?

I suggest you read Section I first to be aware of what's brewing on the horizon.

Awareness precedes change.

Section II outlines the five ways to futureproof your career. You will learn how to become...

- A fully unleashed human to thrive in the era of AI
- A catalyst for change to set you apart from your peers
- An alchemist to transform ordinary into extraordinary
- A captain with nerves of steel to navigate through turbulent times ahead
- A futurist to predict and prepare for the future

Section III outlines the five ways to futureproof your company. You will learn how to...

- Transform your business digitally to stay relevant
- Infuse purpose that guides your company as the true North
- Unleash the spirit of innovation to be a disruptor
- Inspire learning to groom the workforce of tomorrow
- Enjoy expedition by engaging your employees

Whether you are interested in futureproofing your career or your company, make sure to read all chapters in the selected section.

Why?

Because the future is multidimensional.

That's why the book is multidimensional. The book's key theme is that you can't just master one theme, one dimension, and ignore the rest. You have to fire up all your cylinders.

To claim the future, you must evolve multidimensionally. You must evolve holistically.

Speaking of evolving, Alaska's salmon and Florida's green lizards aren't the only species who have been successful at it. There are others.

Take New York City's bedbugs as an example.

Sixty years ago, pesticides nearly eradicated them. But they are back with a vengeance.[4]

Recently, New York City was declared among the top ten most bedbug-infested cities in America.

How did these invaders stage such a heroic come-back? By developing a thicker skin and stronger nerve cells resistant to pesticides.

Today, these bedbugs are 250 times more resistant to pesticides than their ancestors of just a few decades ago.

They are changing, evolving, and adapting rapidly.

Are you?

They would impress Einstein.

Would you?

Would you like to?

Good. Reading this book will help.

SECTION I

THREE DISRUPTIVE FORCES

In this section, we dive deep into each of these disruptive forces:
Artificial Intelligence, Digital Natives, and the Gig Economy.

You will learn:
- How powerful are these forces?
- Why should you pay attention to them?
- How will they impact your career and the company over the next decade?

CHAPTER 1

ARTIFICIAL INTELLIGENCE

> *"If I had asked people what they wanted, they would have said faster horses."*
> Henry Ford

"In 50 years, every street in London will be buried under nine feet of manure," wrote London-based newspaper The Times in 1894.[1] (And you think the news stink these days!)

The prediction referred to a growing crisis in the late 19th Century. The situation was alarming for many large cities in the world that utilized horses as the primary mode of transportation.

New York City had over 100,000 horses (approximately one horse per acre) and faced the brunt of the potential damage. Each horse generated roughly 30 pounds of waste and two gallons of urine a day (you do the math for 100,000 horses).

One commentator predicted that by 1930, horse manure would reach Manhattan's third-story windows.[2]

When delegates from around the world gathered in New York to attend the world's first international urban planning conference in 1898, what do you think was the most pressing issue confronting them? You guessed it right.

The attendees argued and debated for hours at a time. But unfortunately, they couldn't find a solution to the problem. They were resigned to the fact that cities needed horses. With horses came manure.

The conference was supposed to last for ten days. Frustrated, attendees left after only three days.

Yet, within two decades, the problem was solved by an invention that took place over 4000 miles away from New York City. In 1870, Julius Hock of Austria built the first internal combustion engine that ran purely on gasoline[3] (and perhaps more importantly, didn't create manure).

This kicked off a series of technological innovations that changed the transportation industry forever.

In 1886, Henry Ford built his first automobile.

By 1900, there were 8,000 cars in the USA.

In 1906, Alabama set a state maximum speed limit to 8 miles per hour (Imagine the traffic!).

By 1908, there were as many cars as there were horses in New York City.

By 1917, the last horse-drawn trolley in New York City was retired.

And just like that, in less than twenty years, automobiles had displaced the jobs of 100,000 horses in the city.

For close to 4,000 years, horses had become an essential part of our lives, providing the fastest transportation mode everywhere. In villages. In farms. In cities. On the battlefields.

They were indispensable. *Until they were not.*

Within years, they were rendered jobless by innovation, by new technology.

Do humans have a lesson to learn from horses?

One of the headlines in a recent issue of Economist asked the ominous question, "Will robots displace humans as motorized vehicle ousted horses?"

The question is not new, nor is it unfounded.

It has popped up after every industrial revolution for the past 250 years.

While the past three industrial revolutions increased productivity, enhanced prosperity, and expanded the economy, each of them caused massive disruption to the prevailing job market. And each time, millions of workers got the short end of the stick.

The first industrial revolution used newly discovered steam power to mechanize the textile production. This enhanced workers' productivity in England and grew the local economy. But the workers didn't benefit much from it as their income remained stagnant for over 50 years.[4]

The second industrial revolution used electricity to power assembly lines in factories. It used gasoline to power automobiles. This resulted in one of the biggest job displacements within the US. Over 100 years, 90 percent of the farmworkers in the US lost their jobs.[5] Despite this, the economy continued to grow as millions of new jobs were created, mainly in the manufacturing sector.

The third industrial revolution utilized information technology and computers to automate factories. History repeated itself. In 60 years, 75 percent of the people working in the manufacturing industry lost their jobs. The economy continued to grow as new technology improved productivity and created millions of new jobs in the service sector.

The fourth industrial revolution is here

Powered by unprecedented computing power, availability of seemingly unlimited data, and increasing adoption of artificial intelligence, the fourth industrial revolution is gaining momentum.[6]

Once again, we find ourselves confronting the difficult questions.

How many jobs will be lost due to the increased use of artificial intelligence?

Would the new jobs created in other sectors make up for the lost jobs?

OR

Is this time different?

What if artificial intelligence continues to get better not only at doing routine and predictable tasks but also at cognitive tasks? What if there aren't enough jobs left for humans to do anymore?

In 1930, a renowned economist John Maynard Keynes predicted his grandkids would be working 15 hours a week as technology increased prosperity and lowered drudgery (well, that clearly hasn't happened yet. If anything, it's more like 15 hours a day).

But what if his prediction comes true for his great, great, grandkids?

The answers to these questions depend on our time horizon. How far out in the future are we looking at? Are we looking at 10 years out, 50 years out, 100 years out, or even more?

If there is no defined time horizon, this chapter may turn into science fiction. Like when the superintelligence system (Skynet from Terminator) ends the human race.

We will avoid going down that rabbit hole. Instead, we will focus on how AI will likely impact your career and your company in the decade ahead.

Invisible and Omnipresent Force

Thanks to Sci-fi novels and movies, when we think about AI, we think of elusive futuristic technology.

We think of ultra-intelligent humanoid robots.

We think of the future, not the present.

And yet, AI is here today. And it is everywhere.

We don't see it or feel it or notice it because AI is working its magic in the background.

Mark Weiser, a computer pioneer, once famously said, "The most profound technologies are those that disappear. They weave themselves into the fabric of everyday life until they are indistinguishable from it."

AI is profound.

Just like electricity, it permeates throughout our lives, and it's so deeply embedded that we don't even think about it.

When you wake up in the morning and unlock your smartphone using Face ID, or at the end of your day, when you are watching one of the "recommended for you" movies on Netflix, are you aware that AI is the thing doing its magic behind the scene?

And during the day, while you are going about your life, have you ever wondered...

Who is curating my social media timelines and notifications?
Who is predictively giving me options as I type my Google search?
Who is categorizing my Gmail box and providing me with smart and contextual replies?
Who is choreographing my commute to work with the recommended route and travel time?
Who is blocking my credit card or alerting me by a text message to prevent fraud?
Who is concocting a personalized playlist for me on Spotify?
Who is creating a beautiful bokeh effect when I take a portrait photo on my smartphone?

And in the near future, when you will receive an item from amazon *even before you buy it*, who will be reading your mind?

The real question, of course, is not "Who?" but "What?"

Will AI take your job?

There is a dichotomy in how we view AI in our lives.

As consumers, we love and embrace these endless manifestations of AI enriching every part of our lives. But, as employees and employers, we become uneasy and anxious about the very thought that it has the potential to significantly alter or completely eliminate our jobs and companies.

The recent media headlines add to this anxiety by featuring multiple studies about how AI will impact our jobs in years to come.

The interest in this topic peaked with a study published in 2013 by researchers at Oxford University. It estimated that around 47 percent of US employment has a high risk of automation over the following two decades.[7]

In 2017, McKinsey came out with its own forecast with a twist. It predicted that 50 percent of current *work activities* (not jobs) are technically automatable by adapting currently demonstrated technologies.[8]

In 2019, Brookings Institution published a study that analyzed an overlap between more than 16,000 AI-related patents and more than 800 job descriptions.[9] It was the first study that concluded that highly educated, well-paid workers may be heavily affected by the spread of AI. This was in direct contrast with almost all other studies that predicted that AI will impact the low wage, low-skilled workers the most.

Each of these studies used a different methodology and came to different conclusions for how many jobs will be impacted, what kinds of jobs will be impacted, and when the jobs will be impacted.

But they all pointed to the same common-sense insight.

Advantage AI

If any task you do as a part of your job is routine, boring, and predictable, AI can do it.

If it has a well-defined objective and a large set of historical data to train AI with, AI can do it.

If it involves basic cognitive functions such as learning, reasoning, problem-solving, and predicting, AI can do it.

Over the years, as we witnessed an increased use of robotics in manufacturing plants, we accepted the fact that AI and robotics can excel at replacing our hands and our bodies, eliminating thousands of blue-collar jobs.

But, with advances in various AI disciplines such as deep learning and computer vision in the recent past, AI has started to replace not just our hands and bodies but also our heads.

AI is color blind.

It doesn't discriminate against blue-collar or white-collar jobs. It infiltrates *any-collar job* where it can do it better, faster, smarter, and cheaper than we can.

One of the best ways to illustrate and expand on this important point is by reviewing real-life examples of how AI is currently impacting the jobs and activities we do in various industries.

As you read through the examples curated below, ask yourselves…

How is AI impacting the jobs and/or the tasks done by humans in each instance?
Is it completely eliminating those jobs and tasks?
Is it assisting and augmenting humans in a given task?
Is it freeing up humans from the grunt work so they can do other value-added work?

Food industry

In 2019, McDonald's acquired two companies.[10]

Two AI startups.

Apprente offers a speech-based AI that converts "speech into meaning" versus "speech into text." Why did McDonald buy this company? To capture your drive-thru order. We all know how annoying it is to have to repeat our order. Well, now we have one less thing to be annoyed about. *Apprente* accurately captures your order the very first time regardless of your accent or background noise.

Dynamic Yield provides Amazon-style personalized experience in a drive-thru setting. It tailors the digital drive-thru menu to weather, current restaurant traffic, and trending items. It also recommends additional items based on what you have already chosen. A little more sophisticated than "Would you like fries with that?"

AI is even helping with basic food preparations. For example, Flippy, an AI-powered kitchen assistant from Miso Robotics, is already flipping burgers and frying French fries at a number of burger joints in the US. Unlike a traditional robot, it's connected to Miso AI cloud platform and continuously improves its performance and skills over time.[11]

The best part about Flippy? One hundred thousand hours of continuous uptime. Yup. Good luck getting your photo on the "Employee of the Month" board!

Hotel industry

It's touted as "The Hotel of the Future." When you arrive at the FlyZoo hotel in Hangzhou, China, you hardly see any staff in the lobby.[12] Or even during your entire stay.

The hotel allows you to make reservations and settle bills using a mobile app. When you arrive at the hotel, you check in using self-service kiosks and enter your room using face recognition technology.

Once in the room, a voice-activated assistant is at your service. It will change room temperature, close the curtains, adjust the lighting, and order room service. And guess who delivers your food to your room? A robot.

If you had a long travel day and head to the lobby bar to have a drink, there is no bartender to chitchat with. A robot behind the counter is mixing your cocktails.

The FlyZoo hotel is not the only one embracing this human-free business model. Worldwide, many other hotels (such as Hilton and Radisson Blu) are starting to assimilate the AI-powered automation in their business models.

Retail industry

If you don't like standing in long lines at the check-out counters (or even self-scanning items) at a grocery store, you will enjoy the future.

Amazon Go stores have completely eliminated the need for cashiers and the need to even self-scan the items you want to buy. You walk in the store, grab whatever you want from the shelves, and simply walk out the store. In the background, AI, supported by cameras and sensors, tracks what you bought and charges your Amazon account.

Walmart is automating the way it restocks its shelves. It has deployed AI-powered robots to move through aisles of their giant centers and scan the shelves to identify items that need restocking or are mislabeled.

Zara uses robots to facilitate pick up of the orders done online. When you get to the store, you just key in your pickup code, which triggers a robot to locate the item from the warehouse and to deliver it via a drop box.

Customer Service industry

The omnipresent Chatbots! But they are just a very small part of how AI is revolutionizing the industry.

Companies like Avaamo offer conversational IVR, which not only understands the words the customer is saying but also the meaning, nuance, and the intent behind the question.[13]

There is no need for you to press any button during your IVR experience, as the natural language processing algorithm automatically understands what you are saying and responds accordingly. During the call, it offers additional information to customers via digital channels such as SMS or mobile web, hoping to resolve the customer's issue at a lower cost and more interactive channels. The goal is to resolve as many customer issues without having to engage a live agent.

But even when a call ends up with a live agent, AI plays a significant role by augmenting the agent's performance by updating customer records. This is done by providing highly relevant data points in real-time so agents can answer customer queries and offer personalized solutions to the customer based on their purchase history and past support requests.

Legal industry

If you think highly specialized fields such as law would be immune to AI, you are in for a surprise.

Companies like LawGeex are developing an AI-driven process that can review proposed legal contracts, analyze them using natural language processing, and determine which portions of the contracts are acceptable or not.[14]

Companies like Casetext are tackling arguably the most cumbersome and time-consuming part of a law firm — legal research.[15] They deploy natural language processing to truly understand the legal opinion's actual meaning. They are significantly reducing the need for junior lawyers or paralegals. Over 4,500 US law firms are already using this service.

Healthcare industry

Meet Angel. Appropriately named for a virtual nursing assistant. A bot product of Care Angel, she is available to answer patient's questions 24/7/365.[16] She makes intelligent and personalized care calls to care recipients, provides automatic digital alerts to clinicians when intervention is required and informs loved ones about the care's key elements.

Over time, the machine learning algorithm enables conversations to become more tailored and personalized to an individual. The algorithm also helps determine what will be an effective way of engaging with a particular patient.

The technology's underlying idea is to ensure the patient and the provider remain in contact in-between doctor visits to successfully reduce hospital readmission.

Computer Aided Detection (CAD) is currently being reviewed for a variety of imaging studies. For mammography, it's used to identify areas suspicious of breast cancer for the radiologists to assess further. In fact, in early 2020, Google Health announced that its AI model read mammograms with fewer false positives and fewer false negatives than human experts.[17]

There are plenty of other examples. But you get the drift.

To summarize, if any of the activities you do as a part of your job is boring, repetitive, and predictable (such as flipping burgers, checking in guests at a hotel, answering basic customer queries, and stocking shelves), AI can do it.

If it has a well-defined objective and a large set of historical data to train AI with (such as reading Mammograms, taking drive-thru orders), AI can do it.

If it involves basic cognitive functions, such as learning, reasoning, problem-solving, and predicting (such as offering a personalized drive-thru menu, virtual nurse assistant providing real-time alerts to a doctor, and conducting legal contract reviews), AI can do it.

Advantage Human

So then, what about us?

What jobs would be left for us to do?

The better question to ask is, *what tasks* (that you do within your job) will be left for you to do?

The good news is — at least for the next 10 years — there are plenty of tasks where we will have an inherent advantage against AI.

AI can match our body and, to a degree, our mind. But we have the advantage of having a heart and a conscience.

Both humans and machines can be goal-driven. But only humans know how *to lead and inspire* others to achieve the goal collectively.

Both humans and machines can diagnose diseases. But only humans know how to break the news to the patient with *empathy*.

Both humans and machines know how to excel in a predictable, repetitive environment.

But only humans know how to navigate *unexpected, unprecedented, unpredictable* situations (remember Covid19 crisis?).

Both humans and machines can follow a well-defined, rule-based environment to make a product. But only humans can *create* something completely new, something original in an unstructured, undefined environment.

So, what gives us the edge against the smart machines?

Our creativity, our intuition, our ability to think and act strategically and holistically; our ability to be resourceful and adaptable in unexpected situations; our ability to connect and influence; our ability to lead and inspire others; our ability to empathize and to feel others' pain or joy, and our ability to manifest love.

In 2017, at an expo in Japan, a humanoid robot "Pepper" was introduced as a priest for hire to lead funeral rites.[18] It was programmed to deliver a sermon and chant sutras while tapping a drum.

Intrigued by this news, one of the local Buddhist priests came to see if the robot can "impart heart" because he believed "heart is the foundation of religion."

Pepper has yet to be hired for a funeral.[19]

CHAPTER 2

DIGITAL NATIVES

> *"The past is the prologue."*
> Shakespeare

"Are your children overloaded with information?" read one of the recent headlines in Psychology Today. Another one from CNN blared, "Information overload is driving us crazy."

Even scholars chimed in.

In his book, *Bibliotheca Universalis*, a renowned Swiss scientist and a polymath, Conrad Gessner described how the overabundance of data was both "confusing and harmful" to the mind.[1]

Gessner died in 1565.

He was not referring to the information overload in the digital age. He was referring to the *invention of the printing press* and how *books* were creating information overload for the general population.

Can you imagine?

Gessner grew concerned about the demise of solitude when there were only 10,000 books in the world! Today, there are over 130,000,000 published books in the world.

Every time a new technology (such as the printing press, the radio, the TV, or even the Internet) is introduced, history tends to repeat itself.

The past becomes a prologue.

The older generations, with their outdated frame of reference, are overwhelmed by its potential negative effects. They want to be rooted in the *past* and *stay* there in their comfort zone.

Meanwhile, the younger generations who grow up with the new technology are excited about its limitless potential. They want to build the bridge to the *future* and *go* there. They want to explore and to expand.

Today, as we embrace the new decade, we must unleash the digital native's full potential.

After all, we need a bridge to the digital future. And they know how to build it.

We are headed to the future where *everything* is smart, embedded with *intelligence*. Where we collaborate with AI as much as with fellow humans. Where "innovate or die" is not just a catchy phrase but a stark reality.

This digitally driven future yearns for generations who are digitally fluent.

The generations who are at ease in a world where an AI, like Alexa and Google, augments their reality.

The generations who inherently understand why new products go from being a fad to obsolescence in a matter of months.

The generations who are self-starters and life-long learners.

The generations who are hyper-connected and hyper-cognitive, enterprising and entrepreneurial.

The generations who are confident and curious, fast and furious.

The generations we call Millennials and Gen Z.

Meet Millennials and Gen Z

Millennials (those born between 1980 and 1996) witnessed the arrival and spectacular growth of the Internet.[2]

They became the early adopters and avid users of social media, search engines, instant messaging, smartphones, mobile technology, and AI-powered personal assistants. They outshined and outpaced Gen Xers and Baby Boomers with their fluency in this rapidly evolving digital world.

Gen Z (those born between 1997 and 2012) took it a few notches higher! Unlike Millennials, the youngest generation wasn't just a spectator to the technological revolution, they were born into it.

They got their first smartphone when they were just a little over 10 years old. For them, the Internet, Facebook, smartphones, high definition, streaming, and Siri were not inventions, but the reality that they called life.

So why should you pay attention to them? For three main reasons.

One, for their sheer numbers. Gen Z is now the largest generation in the world, with 2.47 billion people (Millennials following closely at 2.4 billion people).[3]

Two, they are joining the workforce on a massive scale. By 2030, as the last batch of Baby Boomers reaches the retirement age of

65, these young generations will become the largest segment of the world's workforce.[4]

In the US, they will make up two-thirds of the total workforce. While in countries with large and growing young populations like India and China, their workforce participation will be even higher.

Three, these young generations are radically different because of their immersive upbringing in a rapidly evolving digital world. Even before they need a job, they have cultivated skills that are any employer's dream!

What makes them radically different?

They are savvy brand builders. With a highly curated presence across social media, personal websites, and apps, they are the de facto mini-CEOs of their personal brands.

They are global. They seek out and thrive in communities of like-minded people, based not just in their neighborhoods or cities, but across the globe.

They are resourceful. Thanks to Google and YouTube, these adolescents can learn anything they want in a matter of minutes.

They are entrepreneurial. They know how to enhance a business plan through crowdsourcing and then manifest it through crowdfunding.

Clearly, their readiness to hit the ground running in the job market is unprecedented.

Every young generation in history was born into new technology like the wheel, printing press, and steam engine. While these powerful innovations were game changers, they were not an integral part of our daily lives. They also didn't influence how kids prepared for their careers.

For example, a wheel was a revolutionary innovation. But kids didn't spend hours glued to it. It was not a portal to limitless knowledge, connections, and possibilities.

This is the first time the new technology, deeply interwoven in our daily life, is democratizing information, power, and hence *possibilities*.

Anyone (regardless of age, location, or social standings) with a great idea and deep understanding of how the digital world works has the opportunity to find success.

Zooming in on the most crucial and disruptive differences

If you Google "Millennials" or "Gen Z," you will get more than 100 million search results featuring blogs, news articles, podcasts, videos, and books.

These generations have been under the microscope since birth, and every aspect of their lives has been dissected (literally, every aspect).

Your Google search may turn up the survey that asked Gen Z, "if you were given a choice between a working Wi-Fi or a working bathroom, what would you choose?" (40 percent would choose a working Wi-Fi.)[5]

Your Google search will also dig up plenty of articles about how and why they are so narcissistic and self-centered. But let us remind ourselves that the clichéd term "Me Generation" was not coined for Millennials. It was first used in the 70s for Baby Boomers.[6] Every generation, when young, tends to be a bit self-absorbed. Then *life* happens. Humbling us along the way.

So, we should not focus on the differences stemming from their relative youth. Because as they age and mature, these age-related differences (like being self-centered) will fade away (for the most part).

Instead, we should focus on the differences stemming from the unique environment and technological ecosystem they grew up in. And how that experience altered their outlook on what's important, what they value, and who they want to be.

As the CEO of a company where almost 100 percent of the people we hired in the last three years were Gen Z or Millennials, I found myself at Ground Zero of this massive generational shift.

Right up close and personal, I witnessed how radically different these youngsters are from the old guards (like myself).

In particular, there are three characteristics that set them apart:

1. <u>They want to work with the latest technology</u>

In the last decade alone, these digital generations witnessed people upgrading their smartphones every two years.

They witnessed Siri ceaselessly evolving from a mere novelty to an intuitive and intelligent virtual assistant.

They witnessed the speed of Internet connectivity increase by 20-fold.[7]

They only know one way to exist. Upgrade. Get better. Get faster. Get smarter. Repeat.

So it's no surprise that they are picky when it comes to choosing their employer. They are looking for an employer who will provide them with the latest technology to work with.

In a 2018 survey conducted by Dell covering 12,000 Gen Zers from age 16 – 23 from 17 different countries, 80 percent said they want to work with cutting edge technology.[8] And, 91 percent said the technology offered by an employer would be a factor in choosing among similar job offers.

Their penchant for working with the latest technology is also apparent in who they consider as their dream employers. According to Glassdoor's study in 2019, both Gen Z and Millennials chose tech giants such as IBM, Google, Microsoft, and Amazon among their top ten choices.[9]

So, there you have it. This is what you are up against.

Now, granted, not every company can be a Google or Amazon.

But, every company can ensure its technology meets the demands of its customers and employees of *tomorrow*.

Every company can provide the technology that promotes a fluid and personalized work environment, where one can work from anywhere, and at any time.

The one that simplifies and automates employee-facing processes to match "there is an app for that" mindset of young generations.

The one that adapts to humans, unlike the frustrating "take it or leave it" legacy systems.

The one that leverages tools to unleash the collaborative spirit of young generations.

2. They are entrepreneurial

Do you know Charli D'Amelio, Baby Ariel, or Jacob Sartorius? If not, you are not alone. I had to Google them myself.

They are outrageously popular celebrities. And perhaps the reason you haven't heard of them is that they found their stardom not in movies or TV series but on relatively new platforms like TikTok and musical.ly.

But don't let that discount their star power. Charli alone has over 87 million followers on TikTok, and that's growing by the day.

And guess what? All three of them were born after 2000.

What's even more impressive is that, like true entrepreneurs, they have turned their enviable following on social media into a lucrative business. They are signing sponsorship deals, releasing their music albums, and landing prominent roles in popular TV series and movies (and even appearing in super bowl commercials).

They are not alone. There are countless others pursuing their passion. Making money by doing what they love to do. Their motto (in Gen Z speak): "You do you."

Like Charli, many of them followed the path of music and entertainment through TikTok, musical.ly, and YouTube.

But many others launched their businesses by creating an app, running an online creative agency, or even buying and selling sneakers online.

Why are young people more likely to become an entrepreneur today? Because it is much easier for them to start a business in their youth than any other generation.

What do you need to start most businesses today? Of course, an amazing idea. But what else? *A smartphone and Internet connectivity.* Talk about almost no barrier to entry.

This easy access has influenced how young generations envision living their lives. A recent study found that 72 percent of high schoolers want to start their own business someday, and 61 percent of college students would rather be entrepreneurs than employees.[10]

So, if you are an employer trying to hire these young people, you are competing with not only other employers but also their desire to be the masters of their own destiny.

Even if you are lucky to hire them, retaining them is equally difficult.

They won't survive too long in companies where the bosses at the top make the decisions and micromanage the rest to carry them out.

Where new ideas are met with "this is how we have always done it."

Where they are asked to fit their square peg in a round hole.

Where management is obsessed with employees putting in their hours rather than their *hearts and souls*.

3. <u>They are purpose-driven</u>

Yes, they have gained their notoriety for being an avocado toast loving, soy latte-drinking, TikTok-ing, Snapchatting generation. But if you look beyond this narrow and myopic stereotype, you realize that these digital generations are the most woke and inspired generations to tackle the urgent social and environmental issues facing the world today.

According to a 2019 study conducted by Porter Novelli/Cone, 88 percent of Gen Zers feel their generation has the power to transform the world for the better.[11] And it's not because they are naïve. But because they have seen young people *their age* making a difference on a global scale.

They have proudly witnessed Malala Yousafzai (a fellow Gen Zer and the youngest recipient of the Nobel Peace Prize) continue to fight for women's and children's rights. Despite receiving the death threats from the Taliban.

Then there is the "Greta effect." In Greta Thunberg, they see their own limitless power and potential. Yes, it's uplifting when your teacher or a parent reminds you that "you have the power to change the world."

But nothing inspires you more than seeing someone just like you, someone your age, someone as vulnerable as you are, *take on* the world for a cause she believes in. It emboldens, empowers, and energizes you.

They have also come to recognize that they can't wait for grown-ups to fix the issues near and dear to their heart.

This was evident after the high school shooting in Parkland, Florida. The surviving students took matters in their own hands and made an impassioned plea to the world to protest against gun violence.

And people of all ages listened. Nearly 800,000 people from all across the US turned up in Washington DC to participate in the *March For Our Lives* (800 similar marches were organized in cities worldwide).[12]

These young generations know they have the *muscle to morph mobile messages into movements.*

So, what does this mean for you as an employer?

It's simple.

Young people are looking for employers who are equally engaged in and committed to solving social and environmental issues near and dear to their hearts. Just consider these numbers:

Eighty-three percent of Gen Zers believe a company's purpose is a core consideration for deciding where to work.

Seventy-five percent of the millennials would take a pay cut to work for a socially responsible company.

And no, they won't take your word for your Corporate Social Responsibility (CSR). They are a skeptical bunch. They want to know if you are putting your money where your *values* are.

So, if your CSR program is an afterthought, if it doesn't permeate throughout the entire company, if it's relegated to a person or a team, if it *comes to life* only in a paragraph of your annual report, it won't survive the sniff test.

Here is the bottom line: People won't commit to your brand until you commit to your social responsibility.

In the world we live in, companies should not have a CSR strategy.

CSR should be *the* strategy.

In 1970, Milton Friedman, a renowned economist, wrote an essay in the New York Times Magazine titled, "The social responsibility of business is to increase its profits."[13] He argued that a company has no social responsibility to the public or society; its only responsibility is to its shareholders.

Needless to say, he hadn't met the Millennials and Gen Z yet.

CHAPTER 3

THE GIG ECONOMY

> *"The secret to happiness is freedom."*
> Thucydides

"I offered Richard the service of free lances, and he refused them," said a feudal lord referring to the paid army he has assembled in Sir Walter Scott's novel *Ivanhoe*.[1] "I will lead them to Hull, seize on shipping, and embark for Flanders; thanks to the bustling times, a man of action will always find employment."

This was one of the earliest written evidence of the word "freelance." The 1819 novel used the term to refer to a medieval mercenary or a soldier who would fight for whichever kingdom paid him the most.

With Germanic and French roots, the word "Freelance" loosely means "one who loves to hurl, to throw, or to discharge." So, essentially, a mercenary who loved to hurl, throw, or discharge weapons.[2]

Today's modern-day mercenaries (now commonly known as the freelancers) are still "fighting" for the one who pays. The kind of war they wage, however, has changed.

Who they are fighting for has changed from kingdoms to companies.

What they are fighting for has changed from land-grab to market-grab.

What they are fighting *with* has changed from physical weapons to the digital ones.

What is *at stake* has changed from potentially dying on the battlefield to receiving a one-star review on an online marketplace (a fate worse than death!).

But there is one thing that hasn't changed over the centuries. A penchant for freedom.

Freedom to do what they love to do. Freedom to choose who they do it for. Freedom to choose for how long.

As the digital generations storm the workforce over the next decade with their insatiable craving for autonomy, *freedom has become the new currency*.

And people want more of it.

One would think that if the secret to happiness is freedom, freelancers should be happier than traditional workers. Are they?

Evidently, yes.

A study done by McKinsey Global Institute in 2016 found that the freelancers report higher levels of satisfaction than traditional workers.[3]

It revealed freelancers fared better in twelve out of fourteen aspects of their work-life, such as the level of empowerment, the creativity one can express at work, flexibility on where to work as well as how many hours to work. Additionally, they had higher positive attitudes toward the opportunities to learn, grow, and develop and the level of income (in the remaining two aspects — income security and benefits — their satisfaction was not significantly different from those who were freelancing by choice).

A study done by Management School and the University of Exeter in 2018 covering 5,000 workers in the UK, US, Australia, and New Zealand confirmed that self-employed people are happier and more engaged at work than those traditionally employed.[4]

Another survey, conducted by AND.CO in 2017, found that 68 percent of freelancers said their quality of life has improved since going independent.[5]

Evidently, Thucydides was right. The key to happiness is freedom.

He had also pronounced a sequel. "The key to freedom is courage."

So, how many brave souls (striving for happiness) have the courage to leave behind the comforts, safety, and financial security of a boring 9-to-5 drudgery for an exciting, fulfilling, and happy freelancing life often punctuated with financial uncertainties and insecurities?

More and more. Every single day.

Freelancing is in vogue

According to the "Freelancing in America: 2019" study, which surveyed more than 6,000 US workers, 35 percent of the US workforce is engaged in freelancing (which is about 57 million people!).[6]

What's noteworthy is that between 2014 and 2019, the period when the job market was increasingly tightening, the unemployment rate was approaching its historical low and when people had plenty of full-time jobs to choose from, 4 million people opted to cut the safety net and embrace the freelancing world.

Freedom is appealing.

It's also addictive.

Once you have tasted how sweet it is, it's hard to imagine living without it. In fact, 51 percent of the freelancers said *no amount of money* would entice them to traditional employment.

This is true for low-skilled jobs like dog walkers and Uber drivers, but also those with advanced degrees.

In fact, skilled professionals make up 45 percent of this market.

These are the professionals in computer programming, marketing, IT, business consulting, writing, graphics, legal, and accounting, to name a few — many with advanced degrees.

You will even find a few Harvard MBAs and even a graduate of Harvard Law School promoting their services on Upwork as freelancers (whether you can afford them is a different story).

A global phenomenon

While the US leads with the highest number of freelancers today, it's the rest of the world — especially the developing countries — that will propel freelancing growth in the future.

In 1991, when I was completing my engineering degree in India, like many of my classmates, my fervent wish was to migrate to the US. After all, it was considered the land of opportunities — a place where people went to pursue and manifest the so-called American Dream.

I vividly remember lining up at 5 am on a cold December morning outside the American Consulate in Mumbai. I remember fervently praying while waiting for my visa interview.

Some five hours later, my turn came, and when the consular officer said the magic phrase, "please pick up your passport tomorrow after 3 pm," I almost jumped with joy. (If it was not for the bulletproof glass separating us, I would have reached over and given my interviewer a big hug!)

It was a life-changing moment for me.

But today, thanks to technology, a visa stamp is no longer the only life-changing moment unlocking new opportunities. Simple Internet access, when used wisely, can change your life.

Basically, the "American Dream" has gone digital and global.

It's no longer about where you go to explore the opportunities in the world. *It's about how you explore the world of opportunities from where you are.*

Imagine. If you are a skilled professional in India, Philippines, Kenya, or anywhere else in the world, you no longer have to line up outside an American Consulate at 5 am. You no longer have to leave your family, friends, home, culture, traditions, and favorite food behind. You no longer have to migrate to a place thousands of miles away.

With access to a personal computer or a tablet and Internet connectivity, you can pursue your American Dream, anytime, anywhere (maybe this is why that iconic disc-mailing company called it America Online so many years ago!).

We are not talking about some futuristic scenario here. This is happening now.

Many prominent platforms in the freelancing industry are connecting employers and freelancers from every corner of the world. For example, the company Freelancer claims they connect 44 million employers and freelancers from over 247 countries, regions, and territories.[7] Upwork claimed to have 14 million users from 180 countries in 2017. It's safe to assume that number is even higher now.[8]

Granted, if you look at the total global workforce made up of over 3 billion people, the size of the freelancing industry is still not that significant.

But don't let that fool you.

It's the velocity with which it's growing that matters.

Why the future is bright for freelancing

According to the "Freelancing in America" survey conducted in 2017, 50.9 percent of the US workforce will be freelancing by 2027. That's over 25 million more people joining the freelancing bandwagon over the next decade.[9]

The growth rate will be even steeper in developing countries. For example, India is estimated to have 15 million freelancers today.[10] By 2030, that number is expected to grow to 60 million.

What's fueling these freelancing forecasts?

1. Technology makes it easy to freelance and to find a freelancer

Back in medieval times, hustling for a gig was not easy. Often, mercenaries had to travel for weeks, if not for months, before finding a kingdom or a warlord who would hire their services.

Imagine going through all that hassle to find work and then? Risking your life on the battlefield!

Over the years, freelancing became significantly less deadly. But until recently, it remained highly inefficient in how freelancers and clients found each other and how they transacted.

Just 20 years ago, if you were a freelancer, finding a client was hard work. You asked for referrals from family, friends, and existing clients. Whether you liked it or not, you had to attend industry events and gatherings. You gave out business cards and flyers to local businesses. You even sent out direct mail pieces promoting your services within your area. And there was no guarantee any of these hustles would pay off.

If you think finding clients was difficult, consider getting paid.

It was more like pulling teeth.

Best case, you had to wait for months for that check.

Worst case, you had to write it off. You had almost no leverage against bigger businesses.

Thankfully, those days are behind us.

In the last two decades, technological progress coupled with ubiquitous Internet and smartphones have fueled the growth of many online freelancing platforms like Upwork, Freelancer, 99designs, and Toptal.

Just like eBay and Alibaba, these online platforms eliminate the inherent inefficiencies of a physical marketplace. Your scale is as limitless as the Internet. Your reach is the entire planet.

With just a few clicks, freelancers and clients from all corners of the world can find what (and who) they are looking for.

The mutual reviews and star ratings keep everyone on their best behavior (like indulging your Uber driver in a small talk even when you are in no mood to talk to make sure you get that five-star rating).

And the best part? It's hassle-free!

Clients get the services they are paying for, and the freelancers get the money once the job is completed. Immediately! No need for follow-ups and write-offs!

2. <u>It's a win-win for both employers and freelancers.</u>

Employers win because freelancers — as contractual workers — afford them agility and nimbleness. Companies can better navigate through ebbs and flows in the circumstances, both predictable (such as seasonality) and unpredictable (such as unexpected external events).

Employers also benefit from achieving significant cost savings.

By hiring freelancers, companies don't have to pay for employee-related direct costs, such as recruitment, payroll taxes, matching 401(k), and paid time off.

Companies also save on indirect costs, such as rent or lease, utility bills, insurance, and maintenance for office buildings (not to mention the fortune spent on post-it notes and paper clips).

Freelancers win because they have freedom and flexibility to work from wherever and whenever they want.

If you believe you are most productive and most creative at 2 am adorned in your pajamas sitting at the kitchen table, why not? After all, there is no alarm going off at 7 am. There is no need to get ready and commute to work.

You are your own boss!

For freelancers, this freedom also equates to savings.

Working from home means no commute and hence, fewer car-related expenses, such as gas, parking, car maintenance, and car insurance.

Working from home means more time with your kids and hence lower childcare costs (but perhaps more "pulling your hair" moments).

Working from home means no need to buy formal office wear (last time I checked, pajamas are significantly cheaper and more comfortable).

Working from home means that the Starbucks on the corner is no longer tempting you daily to buy a $5 latte!

Working from home means no weekly after-work happy hours (with the people you can't stand).

So, yes, when you add all of these up, it's a nice chunk of savings.

In addition to these savings, probably the biggest win of being a freelancer is not having to deal with a toxic work environment. A recent survey done by Perkbox in the UK found the primary cause for work-related stress is not being over-worked. It is office politics.[11]

Freelancers don't have to put up with that nonsense.

No need to be paranoid about backstabbers.

No overzealous colleagues trying to outmaneuver you for a promotion.

No bullies to fend off.

No bosses to suck up to.

(No wonder freelancers are a happier bunch.)

3. <u>Anyone who can use the Internet can become a freelancer</u>

In the last chapter, we discussed at length how the digital generations — Millennials and Gen Z — are entrepreneurial and that a majority of them aspire to start their own business.

Well, they are not kidding.

Gen Z has just started to join the workforce, and 53 percent of these young workers are freelancing. Millennials are not far behind, with 40 percent of these workers working as freelancers.[12]

These numbers are not surprising. After all, when we think of a freelancer, we think of a headphone-wearing, young and scrappy Gen Zer or a Millennial working away at WeWork or Starbucks.

We never think of people in their sixties hustling for gigs, but maybe we should.

Today, 29 percent of the Baby Boomers (currently those 55 or older) in the workforce are freelancing. And their participation rate is expected to increase over the next decade.

We intuitively know what attracts young people to freelancing. Like their familiarity with the on-demand culture, their innate need for freedom and flexibility, and their proficiency in technology fueling the gig economy.

But why are the Baby Boomers turning to freelancing?

Aren't they supposed to retire, walk into the sunset, spend the rest of their days golfing or playing bridge with their friends?

Aren't they too steeped in their rigid 9-to-5 mindset?

Can they adapt to this fast-moving digital economy?

Adapting they are!

Why? Well, some want to. And some have to.

Some want to because they enjoy working. Others realize they don't have the savings they need.

The life expectancy is on the rise globally, and people are living longer and healthier. In the US, 77 percent of workers over the age of 65 said there are no limitations in the kind of work they can do.[13]

Imagine. You have spent 40 years of your life working hard, cultivating skills, gaining experience, garnering wisdom, building a Rolodex, and then boom! Suddenly, just because you reach some arbitrary number, you can't work anymore!

Well, now you can, thanks to freelancing.

And we are not talking about being a greeter at a local Walmart.

We are talking about the kind of work where you can utilize your skills and experience. Or even monetize the life-long passions you have cultivated over the years as a photographer, writer, yoga teacher, or life coach.

Clearly, the stars are aligned for freelancing to take off.

What does this mean for your company?

The increasing popularity of freelancing will alter the future of not just who gets the work done but also where, when, and how.

Companies are familiar with attracting, retaining, training, and developing full-time employees working predominantly from the company premises.

With freelancing on the rise, as leaders, you have to ask yourself:

How would you successfully integrate and leverage freelancers as a part of your HR strategy?

How would you optimize these remote workers?

How would you ensure they work cohesively as one team with your regular employees?

Companies will also be under increasing pressure to retain their full-time employees as freelancing becomes an attractive alternative. You have to ask yourselves:

How can you create a culture that promotes entrepreneurship?

How can you empower your full-time employees to design and manifest personalized career goals?

How can you offer them the freedom, flexibility, and the sense of ownership they crave for?

What does this mean for your career?

As a professional, there has never been a better time to be alive! It has never been easier for you to create and manifest your dreams.

If you feel there is a song in you, it doesn't need to suffocate in a 9-to-5 rat race. You can sing it (and get paid for it!).

Freelancing offers you an option to strike out on your own. Do what you love to do. Minus the noise. Minus the toxicity. Minus the drama.

But, it's not a walk in the park either. While the entire world is your market, the entire world is also your competition. Everyone is hustling for a job or a gig that you want.

So, how do you thrive?

By being at the top of your game. Everyday.

By committing to life-long learning.

By letting go of the past to usher in the future.

By shedding the old to embrace the new.

By learning to unlearn.

To relearn.

SECTION II

FUTUREPROOF YOUR CAREER

In this section, you will learn how to become...

- A *fully unleashed* human to thrive in the era of AI
- A catalyst for change to set you apart from your peers
- An alchemist to transform ordinary into extraordinary
- A captain with nerves of steel to navigate through turbulent times ahead
- A futurist to predict and prepare for the future

CHAPTER 4

THE FUTURE IS AI: BE A HUMAN

> *"Sometimes I just don't understand human behavior."*
> C-3PO, Stars Wars: Episode V, The Empire Strikes Back

Lovotics = Love + Robotics

Corny? Yes, but it exists.

The term "Lovotics" was coined by Dr. Hooman Samani.[1] It refers to the research of human-to-robot relationships and a robot's ability to give love and receive love from humans.

Dr. Samani is the Director of AI and Robotics Technology Laboratory at National Taipei University, Taiwan. He has developed an experimental robot to aid his research.

The robot itself is nothing to write home about. It looks like a furry blob (with less expression than Chewbacca).

But don't let its unimposing exterior fool you. Hidden underneath, there is a sophisticated AI-powered machine.

The robot "feels" human interaction through tactile, visual, and audio sensors. Based on how it feels, its digital endocrine system releases the right mix of digital hormones (such as oxytocin, dopamine, serotonin, and endorphin) into its system. And the infusion of these chemicals alters how it behaves, how it moves, the color of light it emits, and the type of noise it makes.

It's cute and lovable.

But the $64,000 question is: How do you know if the robot loves you too?

Dr. Samani answered this question, "Basically, a robot is a piece of machine. So, we don't care about the feedback [coming] from the robot. We care about this — does the Robot give you the feeling 'that robot loves me'?"

If 15 years from now, my three-year-old daughter Clara tells me that she is in love with someone, my first question to her will be, "Does he (or she) love you too?"

If she gives me this convoluted answer, "the *other person gives her a feeling that he loves her,*" I would ask her to run for her life. (I would probably ask her to run for her life regardless of the answer.)

As humans, we don't have to let others infer whether we love them or not. We express it through our words, gaze, thoughtfulness, kindness, compassion, empathy, understanding, and encouragement.

We know how to love. And we know how to communicate that we love.

AI doesn't.

In October 2018, an artwork — *Portrait of Edmond Belamy* — was sold for $432,500.[2]

Not a big deal.

We are used to rich and famous paying an outrageous amount of money for artworks.

But this particular piece was a big deal.

This painting was "created" by an AI algorithm called GAN, which stands for Generative Adversarial Network, and has two key components: Generator and Discriminator.

The algorithm was fed with a data set of 15,000 portraits painted between the 14th to the 20th Century. The Generator created new portraits based on this vast data set. The Discriminator tried to spot the difference between a human-made portrait and the one created by the Generator.

The goal was to keep creating new images until the Discriminator was fooled into thinking the new image created by AI was actually created by a human.

After a few iterations, the Discriminator was fooled indeed, and that's how we got the pricey portrait.

The news of this auction made headlines around the world.

People wondered if AI can "create" art, what would happen to human artists?

But the question is — did AI really "create" this portrait?

The algorithm was created by humans. The 15,000 portraits from the past were created by humans. Who should take the credit for the creativity? The people who wrote the code for the algorithm? The people who painted those portraits?

No one would give credit to Picasso's brush over Picasso himself.

No one would give credit to Dylan's guitar over Dylan himself.

No one would give credit to Hemingway's typewriter over Hemingway himself.

But in this case, is AI a tool or a personality?

It's confusing. It's hard to answer.

Let's contrast this with the painting "The scream" by Norwegian Expressionist artist Edvard Munch. In 2012, a version of this painting was sold at an auction for nearly $120 million.[3]

Who created it?

Not hard to answer: Munch did.

In his diary on January 22, 1892, Munch described the inspiration: "One evening I was walking along a path, the city was on one side and fjord below. I felt tired and ill. I stopped and looked out over the fjord – the sun was setting, and clouds turning blood red. I sensed a scream passing through the nature; it seemed to me that I heard the scream. I painted this picture, painted the clouds as actual blood. The color shrieked. This became The Scream."[4]

No AI. No Algorithm. No mathematical formula. No data set. No paintings from the past.

Just pure inspiration. From life. From nature. From emotions. From feelings.

Not something out of something. But *something out of nothing*.

Not artificial. But organic.

Not derived. But original.

Humans can be *inspired* to create something *original*.

AI cannot.

In 2014, a team of machine learning specialists at Amazon started to build an algorithm to automate the search for top engineering talent.[5] The company was receiving thousands of resumes and wanted a tool where you feed 100 resumes to it, and it spits out the top five.

The algorithm was fed a data set of resumes submitted over the previous 10 years.

Not surprisingly, in a male-dominated technology field, most of them came from men.

The machine learning algorithm took note of this fact and taught itself that male candidates were preferable. It penalized resumes that included any reference to women. It downgraded graduates of two all-women colleges. It favored words such as "executed" and "captured" — typically found in male engineers' resumes.[6]

The machine learning algorithm did what it was supposed to do. It was learning to become better.

So, it became better.

And in the process, it also became increasingly gender-biased.

So, what went wrong?

Nothing went wrong, except we came face to face with one profound limitation of AI.

It can learn whatever we program it to learn. But it doesn't know whether what its learning is right or wrong.

AI doesn't feel guilt. AI doesn't understand morals.

In this instance, for example, AI, on its own, cannot figure out that it was aggravating gender inequality in the workplace. On its own, it cannot figure out that the world is changing, and the outdated practices of the past are not only politically incorrect but just plain wrong.

As humans, we know what is fair and what is not. We haven't always been fair. History is a witness to our own madness.

But that's different. At least we have a choice. We can choose between being fair or not.

AI doesn't even have a choice.

We have a conscience. We have morals. We have values.

We know what is right and what is wrong.

AI doesn't.

Human beings are complex creatures. Sometimes, even we don't understand human behavior.

Heck, sometimes we don't understand our own behavior, let alone others'.

Why do you think we need therapists?

So, it will be a while before C-3PO and its cohorts will come to understand human behavior. And it may take even longer for them to imitate us.

Until then, there is job security for those who can bring their empathy, creativity, discernment, intuition, and inspiration to work.

Humans and intersections

Dr. Eiji Nakatsu, Director of Technical Development of Japan Railway West, had a problem on his hands.[7] He was getting too many complaints about the bullet train from his staff, passengers, and residents living along the railway track.

The problem was a deafening one. When the bullet train, traveling at over 200 miles per hour, exited the tunnels, it created a loud, deafening sonic boom that could be heard as far as 400 meters away.

Whenever a train, traveling at its maximum speed of over 200 mph, entered a tunnel, it forced the air through the tunnel. Almost as if a piston was moving and pushing the air through a cylinder. The velocity of the train built up the air pressure in waves. When these waves reached the end of the tunnel and released in the open environment, they created a sonic boom.

Dr. Nakatsu needed a solution.

One solution was to reduce the speed of the train. But it was the *speed* that made the train the *"bullet"* train. It's like having Spiderman trying to swing through the air in parachute pants.

So that was a non-starter.

The other solution was preventing the pressure build-up in front of the train by redesigning the nose.

But redesigning the nose to what?

Dr. Nakatsu, an engineer, found the inspiration for this solution in the most unusual place: in his hobby of bird watching.

He observed that when Kingfisher, with its long and pointed beak, dives nose first into water to catch fish, it barely makes a splash. The Kingfisher's beak is a perfect shape for this smooth entry. Why? Because the beak is streamlined. Its diameter steadily increases from its tip to the head.[8]

This aerodynamic shape lessens the impact as the bird easily glides its way into the pond. The water simply flows past the beak rather than being pushed in front of it.[9]

He wondered, what if they replaced the train's bullet-shaped front (which pushed the air forward) with a shape of a Kingfisher beak (which allowed the air to flow past the train)?

He gave it a shot. He gave the train a 50-foot steel "beak."

It worked.

No more sonic boom. No more complaints.

And as a bonus, the train runs 10 percent faster and 15 percent more efficiently.

Where did Dr. Nakatsu find his inspiration?

At the intersection of engineering and ornithology (the study of birds).

Steve Jobs was also a big fan of these intersections.

When he launched the iPad 2, the screen behind him showed a picture of an intersection.[10]

One road sign read Technology and other Liberal Arts. He remarked, "It's in Apple's DNA that technology alone is not enough — it's technology married with liberal arts, married with humanities, that yield us the results that make our heart sing."

He found his genius at these intersections. And he made our hearts sing.

Why is it important for humans to arrive at these intersections?

Because only humans can connect the dots between disparate fields.

AI cannot.

You can build an AI algorithm to identify every single bird in the world with 100 percent accuracy. But Kingfisher's beak won't inspire this algorithm to solve an engineering problem.

You can build an AI algorithm to beat the world chess champion. But the *board-game* won't inspire this algorithm to make a move in the *real-life chess game* played out in the boardrooms.

You can build an AI algorithm to create a new painting. But a painting won't inspire this algorithm to craft a new marketing campaign.

We are different.

We can look at a bird and be inspired to design an airplane. We can watch a sunset and be inspired to paint a masterpiece.

We can look at gecko and be inspired to design a wall-climbing robot. (Not to mention the gecko inspired insurance commercials!).

These intersections differentiate humans from AI.

They expose AI's bounds.

They reveal our boundlessness.

How many roads converge at your intersection?

The Taganskaya Square intersection in Moscow is considered one of the wackiest intersections in the world.[11] It has more than a dozen roads of all sizes merging and intersecting. To navigate through this chaotic maze is so complicated, even Waze probably gets annoyed and loses its temper.

It's no surprise that motorists in Moscow avoid this intersection.

But, metaphorically, we should not avoid it. We should embrace it.

We should aspire to arrive at these wacky intersections of roads we have traveled. And more roads, the better.

"What would you want your kids to become when they grow up?" If you asked this question to any parent when I was growing up in India, almost all of them would have said "doctor or engineer." It made sense then. Parents wanted a better future and financial security for their kids.

But it also meant kids taking a one-lane road in life and sticking to it. It meant these kids grew up to become one-trick-ponies. They mastered the trick. But it was only one trick.

While that formula worked in the past, it doesn't work in this day and age.

Why?

Because AI eats one-trick-ponies for breakfast, lunch, and dinner.

If you are a one-trick-pony, AI can do your job.

If the only trick you know is playing chess, AI will beat you. No matter how good you are. If the only trick you know is being a paralegal, AI will do it better, faster, cheaper, and smarter. No matter how good you are. If the only trick you know is to read X-Rays, mammograms, AI will do it more accurately. No matter how good you are.

But if you have more tricks in your repertoire and you can create something innovative, something unique by combining them, then AI can't touch you.

If you have traveled on many roads and if you know how to create something innovative, something unique at their intersections, then AI can't touch you.

If Leonardo da Vinci were alive today, he would be an enigma to AI.

While he is most known for his paintings (like the Mona Lisa), he had a prolific imagination and an insatiable hunger for learning. During his lifetime, he studied and contributed to the world of sculpture, architecture, music, mathematics, engineering, literature, anatomy, geology, astronomy, botany, paleontology, and cartography.[12]

He was a pony with many tricks. He traveled on so many roads and found many intersections.

He once famously said, "To develop a complete mind, study the science of art, study the art of science. Learn how to see. Realize that everything connects to everything."

If you want to futureproof your career, be what AI cannot be.

Be like Leonardo da Vinci.

Cultivate new hobbies. Learn new skills. Expand your world view.

If you are creative, learn to be analytical. If you are analytical, learn to be creative. Fire up your whole brain — left and right — on all cylinders.

Travel on as many roads as you can and find your own Taganskaya Square. See how everything intersects and connects with everything else.

Someone recently asked me, "What would you like your daughters to become when they grow up?".

It's not as simple as "doctor or engineer" anymore. More than half of the jobs they could be doing 25 years from now are not even invented yet.

So perhaps, "What will they *become?*" is not the right question.

A better question is, "what will they *be?*"

I hope they will be human. *Fully unleashed.*

I hope they will be a pony with many tricks.

Becoming anything will be a breeze, once they have mastered the art of *being human.*

CHAPTER 5

THE FUTURE IS CHANGE: BE A CATALYST

> *"Unless someone like you cares a whole awful lot, nothing is going to get better. It's not."*
> Dr. Seuss, "The Lorax"

No catalysts. No life.

That's the conclusion Dr. Richard Wolfenden came to after years of study.

As a professor of chemistry, biochemistry, and biophysics at the University of North Carolina at Chapel Hills, he knew a thing or two about catalysts. He has been studying them for decades.

In 2008, he discovered something remarkable.[1]

He found that the biosynthesis of hemoglobin and chlorophyll without the catalyst (enzyme) uroporphyrinogen decarboxylase would have a half-life — the time it takes for half of the substance to be consumed — of 2.3 billion years. That's about half the age of the earth.

But in the presence of the catalyst, this reaction happens in mere milliseconds.

It's easy to understand why Scientists like Dr. Wolfenden are fascinated by catalysts. These change agents are minuscule yet so mighty. The survival of life on the planet depends on them.

The rest of us (the non-scientist types) are equally fascinated by catalysts, albeit a different kind.

We may not know what uroporphyrinogen decarboxylase is, how it works it magic, or even how to pronounce it.

But we do know who Rosa Parks is. We do know who Malala Yousafzai is. We do know who Nelson Mandela is. We know how to pronounce their names. And we know how they work their magic to speed up the transformation of our world.

We are fascinated by these human catalysts.

Each one of them so minuscule in the grand scheme of things. And yet so mighty. As Rumi once said, "You are not a drop in the ocean. You are the ocean in a drop."

They inherited a world that needed to change. Segregation. Gender inequality. Apartheid.

They all had a choice: to accept the world as is or be a catalyst and strive to transform it for the better.

They chose the latter.

Was it an easy choice? Was it easy being a catalyst?

No.

Some people didn't like them nor the change they were championing.

Parks lost her job. Yousafzai received death threats. Mandela was imprisoned for 27 years.

But they didn't give in. They knew they couldn't let the world fix itself because they didn't have 2.3 billion years.

So they became the uroporphyrinogen decarboxylase and sped up the transformation.

Dr. Seuss was right. They cared a whole awful lot, and it's because of people like them, things are getting better.

Catalyst = Extraordinary

Parks, Yousafzai, and Mandela were all born into the same ordinary world as millions of other people. But they went on to become extraordinary.

When did their destinies diverge from the masses?

From the moment they witnessed something in their world they didn't like and decided to do something about it.

From the moment they said "no more." No more segregation. No more gender inequality. No more apartheid.

While the masses accepted the world as it was, while the masses resigned to their fate of "it's wrong, but I will live with it," these catalysts chose to envision a better world and strived to manifest it.

So, how do you become extraordinary?

Every time you come across something in your life you don't like or disagree with, you arrive at a fork. There are two paths to choose.

One path says, "it's wrong, but I will live with it." That's the path to ordinary.

The other path says, "no more." That's the path to transforming your world for the better.

That's the path to something extraordinary.

Not everyone who chooses "no more" ends up on the cover of Time magazine. Not everyone gets a Nobel prize.

But that's not a requirement for being extraordinary.

For every Parks, every Yousafzai, every Mandela, there are thousands of unknown, unsung heroes who are choosing the path of "no more" and making a difference in their world. No matter how small it may seem in the grand scheme of things.

You don't have to take on the most pressing sociopolitical issues on a global scale to be extraordinary.

You could be walking on a beach and stumble upon an old can in the sand. You see all the trash lying around. This is your fork.

You can ignore the trash and choose the "it's wrong, but I will live with it" path.

Or you can choose "no more" and do something about it.

Afroz Shah said "no more" and chose to do something about it.[2]

He didn't like the "carpet of plastic" on Mumbai's Versova beach. So, every Sunday morning, he and his neighbor began picking up the trash on the beach. Through social media and word of mouth, he recruited more people to join in his personal crusade. Over the years, Afroz has inspired over 200,000 volunteers to clear more than 60 million pounds of garbage from Mumbai's beaches and waterways.

Has he been on the cover of Time magazine? No.

Has he received a Nobel Prize? No.

Is he extraordinary? Yes.

Just because he chose "no more."

Just because he chose to become a catalyst.

Efren Peñaflorida was born into poverty in the Philippines.[3] His family lived in one of the slums in Manila. In school, he witnessed gangs terrorizing student bodies. Gangs targeting kids hailing from poor families and forcing them to a life of crime, drugs, and violence. He himself became a victim of their bullying.

Efren didn't like what he saw. He arrived at a fork, and he chose "no more."

With his friends, he created the "Dynamic Teen Company" with a mission to provide basic writing and reading skills to kids living on the street. Essentially, giving them a better alternative than joining gangs.

Efren and his volunteers bring pushcarts stocked with books, pens, tables, and chairs into poor neighborhoods and turn them into mobile classrooms. Over the years, they have given better alternatives to over 4,000 underprivileged kids in 38 cities in the Philippines.

Has he been on the cover of Time magazine? No.

Has he received a Nobel Prize? No.

Is he extraordinary? Yes.

Because he chose "no more."

Because he chose to become a catalyst.

Corporate Catalysts

You may not aspire to be the next Rosa Parks or Malala Yousafzai or Afroz Shah. Changing the world may not be your thing. For most of us, it is not.

We simply aspire to excel in our careers and provide a better future for our loved ones.

Is being a catalyst still relevant for us?

Absolutely.

Being a catalyst is not just about transforming the world. It's also about transforming companies.

More than ever before, companies are looking for employees who challenge the status quo.

Employees who don't take "we have always done it this way" for an answer.

Employees who have the courage to say "no more" to the outdated and nonsensical.

More than ever before, companies realize the importance of these "micro" transformers.

Gone are the days when only the CEO championed *once a decade* transformation. Now, every employee must champion transformation every day.

Increasingly, companies are moving their employees from one big and slow mothership to fast and agile speedboats. Companies are empowering their employees with unprecedented autonomy. Companies are pushing decision making to the fringes.

Why are they doing it?

To stay relevant. To survive and thrive. To be better, faster, and smarter.

So, imagine for a second. You are the CEO.

Who would you want as the captains of your speedboats?

Employees who are clocking in their hours with "it's wrong, but I will live with it" mindset?

Or

Employees who are drinking the "No more" Kool-aid?

Take Amazon as an example. How does the company keep reinventing itself every day?

By recognizing that in the 21st century, the CEO cannot be the only catalyst in the company leading change.

When hiring or promoting, Jeff Bezos looks for the "mavericks."[4] He wants to know, "Do they have a pioneering spirit?" He recognizes, "Maybe they are a little bit annoying because they might be a little bit radical. They may not be the easiest people to get along with. But you want them in your organization."

The Amazons of the world know that the only way a company can reinvent itself every day is by hiring and promoting "annoying" catalysts and unleashing their full potential.

You may not be working for Amazons of the world, but you better believe your company is competing with the Amazons of your industry.

Your company has no choice but to adopt the same speed and agility.

Your company has no choice but to hire and promote the "annoying mavericks."

What do mavericks do?

Mavericks like to shake things up.

If they don't like a long and cumbersome recruitment process, they will propose a better one. If they don't like aspects of a company's products and services, they will suggest superior alternatives. If they don't like the customers' user interface, they will advocate for ways to enhance it. If they don't like the outdated business model, they will propose a new one.

The best part is they don't just propose; they infiltrate and influence.

Proposing is easy. Being on the sideline and calling the plays is easy. Being a backseat driver is easy.

Instead, they get in the trenches, work the system, and influence the right people to manifest their ideas. They jump into the arena to create a better product, a better process, a better policy. They get in the driver's seat, delivering an idea to its fruition.

In the decade ahead, being a catalyst will become one of the most highly sought-after skills by the employers.

What does that mean for your career?

The courage to say "no more" will open the door to a "lot more."

Cultivate the catalyst muscles

How do you cultivate the catalyst muscles?

If you have never played tennis, can you play like Serena Williams the first time you hit the court?

If you have never been in water, can you swim like Michael Phelps the first time you jump into a swimming pool?

If you have never held a guitar, can you rock it like Jimi Hendrix the first time you pick up the instrument?

Of course not. Skills are mastered over time. Incrementally.

The same is true for being a catalyst.

You can't live all your life with "it's wrong, but I will live with it" mindset and then one day, show up at work, become a catalyst, and try to transform the company.

You have to purposefully and intentionally cultivate these "catalyst" muscles. Over time.

How do you build muscles for being a catalyst?

Look out for the moments when life presents you with a fork in the road — when you don't like something.

You encounter these moments every day. You just have to be aware of them.

You don't like your kids being bullied in school. You have arrived at a fork. Which path will you take? Do nothing or say "no more," get involved with the school, and be a part of the solution?

You don't like toxic friends in your life. You have arrived at a fork. Which path will you take? Do nothing or say "no more" and find friends who uplift your spirit?

You don't like the lack of work-life balance in your life. You have arrived at a fork. Which path will you take? Do nothing or say "no more" and improve your time management skills?

Ask yourself: what kinds of things are you tolerating in your life that's inconvenient, wrong, or plain sucks?

Start small.

In his book, *Personality Isn't Permanent*, Dr. Benjamin Hardy writes, "If you can't handle the small moments when the stakes are low, you won't show up in the big ones."

Once you learn to say "no more" to the small things, it's easier to say "no more" to the big things.

Every time you choose "no more," two things happen.

One, you strengthen the catalyst muscle. The more you do it, the stronger it gets. Until one day, it becomes a form of muscle memory. It becomes effortless, like riding a bicycle.

Two, you realize the power within you. The power to envision and manifest change. You realize you are not a *creature* of circumstances, but a *creator* of circumstances. You realize you are not defined by what happens to you, but *what you do* with what happens to you.

The more you feel this power within you, the more it empowers you to say "no more" *even more*.

It becomes a part of who you are. A part of your repertoire. A part of your persona.

Be comfortable being uncomfortable

When Savannah — my nine-month-old daughter — was born, she only knew how to lie on her back. Like all babies her age, she didn't stay there. For her, life is not about being at the center of her comfort zone. But it is about being at the edge of it.

It is about pushing her limits and trying new things she has never tried before. Like rolling over, sitting up, crawling, standing up, and soon walking, running, and jumping.

For her, life is about changing and transforming. *Every single day.*

Imagine if babies stayed at the center of their comfort zone forever?

We would still be lying on our backs!

If living in the comfort zone as babies is disastrous for us, why do we do it as adults?

Because as we get older, we get set in our own ways.

We like life to be easy, comfortable, and predictable.

We like life to be the same routine.

We stop looking for challenges.

Same commute. Same Starbucks. Same drink. Same people. Same struggles. Same solutions.

Repeat.

We think this easy, comfortable, and predictable life will never end.

Until the day it does.

Because as the cliché goes, "The only constant in life is change." (Eye-roll inducing but annoyingly true.)

The change disrupts everything.

Life is no longer easy. Life is no longer comfortable. Life is no longer predictable.

We get annoyed. We get upset. We get depressed.

Why is change so painful?

Because we don't want to leave the nice and cozy center of comfort zone and move to the edge.

It's the journey between the center and the edge that's painful.

But what if we don't wait for the change to push us to the edge? What if we go there on our own?

Like babies.

They go through so much change and transformation.

Do they ever get depressed?

Do we have to give them Xanax?

No.

Because they are already living at the edge of their comfort zone. For them, change is not an unwelcome intruder in their life.

For them, *Change is life*.

What if we make *change our life*?

What if we live at the edge of our comfort zone on our own?

How do we do that?

By intentionally breaking our routine.

By intentionally becoming uncomfortable.

By intentionally doing things that will push us out of our comfort zone.

Tim Ferris said so insightfully, "A person's success in life can usually be measured by the number of uncomfortable conversations he or she is willing to have."

Have you been putting off any uncomfortable conversations at home or the office? Go do it.

You think it's hard to learn a new language? Subscribe to Rosetta Stone.

You think you are not creative? Sign up for an art class.

You think you have two left feet? Time to put on your dancing shoes.

Are you afraid of the unfamiliar? Travel to a place where no one speaks your language.

Are you afraid of height? Go bungee jumping.

Why should you intentionally become uncomfortable?

So that being uncomfortable becomes the new normal for you.

So that the change doesn't throw you off your game.

Change becomes your game.

Why is this important?

As a catalyst, you are championing change.

Think about it. How would you inspire others to change if they see you struggling with change? If they see you hyperventilating. If they see you losing sleep over it. If they see you losing your cool.

When you are championing change, you want to be like Parks, Yousafzai, and Mandela.

Be as solid as a rock.

Be as cool as a cucumber.

When Savannah was born, people advised me to be a good role model and teach her good values.

I often heard, "She has so much to learn from the adults around her."

I don't know about that.

But I do know I have so much to learn from her.

Like not lying on my back all day.

Like being comfortable at being uncomfortable.

Like being as solid as a rock.

Like being as cool as a cucumber (unless she is hungry...then, all bets are off!).

CHAPTER 6

THE FUTURE IS PEOPLE: BE AN ALCHEMIST

> *"The real alchemy is transforming base self into gold."*
> Fred Alan Wolf, Author,
> Taking the Quantum Leap

Johann Friedrich Böttger was on the run.

He had escaped the protective custody of the King of Prussia. But the freedom was short-lived. Soon after, he was caught by the King of Poland.[1]

In 1700, the word had gotten out that Böttger — an 18-year-old alchemist — was secretly pursuing a Philosopher's stone, a substance capable of turning base metals into gold.

Once the secret was out, he became a prized target for monarchs. Especially for those — like the King of Poland — whose empires were in financial ruins.

What better way to cure financial woes than to turn any metal into gold?

The King didn't waste any time. He imprisoned Böttger in a dungeon and ordered him to produce "gold making tincture" if he wanted his freedom back.

The young alchemist labored for years. He tried one concoction after the other. But to no avail. Finally, frustrated and disheartened, he gave up his quest.

For Böttger, the Philosopher's stone remained elusive. Transforming base metal into gold remained elusive. Success at alchemy remained elusive.

He is not alone.

Over the centuries, countless others have tried their luck, but they all came home empty.

Alchemy remains the same today as it has been for centuries. A mystical mystery (perhaps Fred Alan Wolf is right).

The real alchemy is not about transforming base *metal* into gold.

The real alchemy is about transforming base *self* into gold.

The real alchemy is about eliciting the very best in us.

The real alchemy is about unveiling the sparkling gold within us.

The gold of greatness.

We don't need to channel Indiana Jones' avatar and go on some mystical adventure to find a philosopher's stone. We don't need to hide in a secret dungeon to concoct the "gold making tincture." There is no tattered map to follow. There are no cryptic clues to decipher.

We just need to look within and unveil the treasure of gold. We just need to remove the veil of mediocrity so that the greatness within us can shine through. Like 24-carat gold.

Once you recognize what lies within us, once you know how to unveil it and let it shine, you morph into an alchemist.

As Russell Conwell wrote in his iconic book, Acres of Diamonds, "Your diamonds are not in far distant mountains or in yonder seas; they are in your own backyard, if you but dig for them."

Once you understand this phenomenon, the world becomes a magical place where...

Mission impossible becomes possible.

Unsurmountable becomes surmountable.

Dream becomes reality.

This is no voodoo science. This is real.

Take President John F. Kennedy, for example.

JFK exhorted the nation to land a man on the moon and bring him back safely by the end of the decade.

Mission impossible? Absolutely.

But he was an alchemist.

His world was a magical place. He knew how to turn a dream into reality. Insurmountable into surmountable. He believed there is limitless potential within each of us. And he knew how to tap into it. He knew how to unveil it so it can shine through.

He assembled the best team from all over the world. He gave them the resources they needed. He empowered them. He made them aware of the gold of greatness lying within them.

When Neil Armstrong became the first human to land on the moon and returned home safely, unfortunately, JFK was no longer around. But everyone working on the Project Apollo shined and sparkled. Like 24-carat gold.

Take Mahatma Gandhi, for example.

He was born into a world where people fought for freedom through war and violence. By shedding blood. By sacrificing lives. But he vowed to embrace non-violence to take on the most powerful empire in the world.

Mission impossible? Absolutely.

But Gandhi was an alchemist.

His world was a magical place. He lived and breathed non-violence in his thoughts, his words, and his actions. His message resonated with millions of people. He recognized and unveiled the greatness within him and those around him.

When India won its independence, these freedom fighters shined and sparkled. Like 24-carat gold.

Take Steve Jobs, for example.

When he returned to Apple in 1996 after 11 years, the company was in dire condition. It was floundering as the market was inundated with cheap PCs. Apple's market cap was a measly $3B (compared to $100B of its nemesis, Microsoft).[2] Jobs aspired to turn the dying business around and reclaim Apple's luster.

Mission impossible? Absolutely.

But Jobs was an alchemist. His world was a magical place.

Unveiling his own greatness, he revamped the company. He created and checked off "what not to do list," shutting down many of the company's failing ventures. He focused the company's energy, efforts, and resources on revitalizing the Mac business and introducing revolutionary products like iPod, iPhone, and App store.

Along the way, he inspired and demanded his team to be the very best they can be. He exhorted them to unveil the greatness within them.

In 2018, when Apple became the first company to reach a $1 trillion market cap, Steve Jobs was no longer around to celebrate this historic milestone.

But thanks to his alchemy, his employees shined and sparkled. Like 24-carat gold.

The likes of Kennedy, Gandhi, and Jobs are not born alchemists. They learn and master the art and science of alchemy.

They know the ingredients for making the gold making tincture.

Five magic ingredients for being an alchemist

1. Redefine limits

Alchemy is not about the past or the present, it's about the future. It's not about "what is" but about imagining "what could be" and achieving it.

If "what is" remains "what is," there is no transformation, no growth, no progress.

The bolder the "what could be," the more profound the transformation, the growth, the progress.

Being a visionary is about aiming for your wildest dream.

It's not about playing small or playing safe.

Instead, it's about playing for what many may declare impossible.

Think about Muhammad Ali's motto: "Impossible is not a fact. It's an opinion."

Elon Musk lives by it and proves it right. Every day.

He sets out to achieve goals that are impossible and outrageously ambitious.

People call him crazy. People mock his vision. People write him off.

In a 2008 article, the New York Times reported that many auto experts doubted whether Tesla could pull off a transition from its expensive sports car to a five-seat, all-electric $60,000 sedan.[3] He let his achievement do the talking. To date, the company has sold close to half a million of these sedans.

When he announced a $35,000 Model 3 for the mass market, people said he would never be able to pull that off. He let his achievements do the talking. In the last three years alone, Model 3 has sold over half a million units.[4]

His vision for SpaceX is even more impressive and far-reaching. He wants to reduce the cost, improve the reliability of space travel, and make it accessible for almost anyone.

The naysayers chimed in again. They said it was impossible.

Musk ignores the noise.

Since sending the first privately funded liquid-fueled rocket to reach orbit in 2008, SpaceX has been inching toward its vision. Most recently, it became the first private company to send humans to the International Space Station in May 2020.[5]

His ultimate goal for SpaceX? To build a colony of humans on Mars.

His ultimate personal goal? To die on Mars.

"I've said I want to die on Mars," Musk told an audience, "just not on impact."[6]

You think he is nuts? He doesn't care.

He lets his achievements do the talking.

As an alchemist, he is transforming people, societies, and the world along the way.

Your vision doesn't need to be about conquering space.

But aim to be the very best at what you do on earth.

Don't try to be the top sales, operations, or marketing team in your company, in your region, in your country. Aim high to be the very best globally. If there was an Olympics for your job, you are shooting for gold.

What is your vision for yourself and your team?

Is it exciting enough for you and your team to get fired up?

Is it bold enough to transform you and your team?

Is it impractical and impossible enough for people to laugh at you?

2. <u>Be authentic</u>

Alchemists come in all sizes and flavors. Some are extrovert, some are introvert. Some are charismatic, some are nerdy. Some are traditional, some are eccentric. Some relish the public persona. Others find bliss in privacy.

But they all have one thing in common. They are authentic. They know who they are.

And most importantly, they are ok being who they are.

They don't compete with anyone or copy anyone. Because doing either means to be defined by someone else's life. It means to reflect someone else's light.

Alchemists know they are unique. They want to shine their own light by simply following their own path. By following their own calling.

They may be oddballs. People may poke fun at them, but they don't try to fit in. They stick to their deep-rooted values and beliefs.

In 1931, when Mahatma Gandhi visited Britain and met with King George V in his signature clothes with bare legs and sandals, he was called a "half-naked fakir."[7] He didn't mind. He remained true to who he was.

Sixteen years later, with his eccentric and authentic persona (and half-naked attire), he brought the great empire to its knees and won India its independence.

We live in a world where there is so much pressure to fit in and conform to unity. Pressure to look, think, act the same.

And yet, paradoxically, we respect people who have the courage to be real. Courage to be who they are. No matter how wacky or weird.

Do you know who you are?

Are you busy competing with others and copying others? Or are you embracing your uniqueness?

Are you letting your authenticity shine through?

Are you letting your own light shine through?

3. <u>Cultivate growth mindset</u>

Humility, derived from the root humus (earth), means "grounded" or "from the earth".

While inspiring leaders float high above the clouds to dream up lofty goals, their feet are firmly planted on the earth.

While they have an ambitious and optimistic view of what they want to accomplish in the future, they have a humble and realistic view of the skills and talents they lack to get there.

They know they have a lot to learn.

When Satya Nadella became the CEO of Microsoft in 2014, the glory days of the company's legacy PC software business were behind it. In a world increasingly dominated by smartphones and tablets, Microsoft was slowly spiraling toward obsolescence.

He knew the company wouldn't survive by resting on its laurels from the past.

Inspired by Carol Dweck's groundbreaking book, "The Growth Mindset," Satya Nadella exhorted Microsoft employees to embrace a new mantra: "Don't be a know-it-all, but be a learn-it-all."[8]

Armed with this new rallying cry, the company cultivated a culture of humility and orchestrated one of the most remarkable turnarounds in modern history. Since 2014, Microsoft's stock price has more than quadrupled.

Are you a "know-it-all" or "learn-it-all?"

Are you busy gloating in the past success or sharpening your saw for the future?

Are your feet firmly planted on the earth?

Do you know the skills and talents you need to achieve your goals?

Are you humble enough to recognize that you won't be able to achieve your goals alone?

4. Jump off the cliff…with them

We live our lives in awe of people jumping off the cliff of complacency and flying.

Flying high.

Like landing a man on the moon and returning him safely. Like winning India's freedom by offering another cheek. Like turning around a company hurtling toward extinction.

We think these people are special. That they are born with wings. That they are born to fly.

And we think without wings, we are stuck on the cliff. We think we are tethered to our safety nets. We think we could never learn to fly.

Until one day, when a teacher or a parent or a mentor or a boss or a coach pushes us off the cliff. We are terrified. We think we will fall.

But we fly.

Those who push us off the cliff are the alchemists.

They know we have wings. They know we can fly.

But they know *we must jump off the cliff first. To fly.*

They know that we must unshackle the chains of complacency holding us down before we can reveal the greatness within.

In 1958, the Green Bay Packers had eight *future* Hall of Famers on their roster, and yet the team ended the season with the worst record in Packers history.[9] This was the 10th consecutive losing season. The team was demoralized. The fans were enraged.

The following year Vince Lombardi was brought in as the head coach. In his first speech to the team, he said, "Gentlemen, we are going to relentlessly chase perfection…I am not even remotely interested in being just good."

When the team started the pre-season training, he pushed them harder, longer, and more intensely than ever before.

One player reminisced, "I've done two boot camps in the Marines. And those didn't even come close to how hard Lombardi's practices were."

The other remembered, "He wanted every ounce of the ability you had, and he wouldn't relent until you gave it to him."

During his nine-year career with the Packers, Lombardi took the team from the worst record in the team's history to five NFL championships and six conference titles.

The Lombardi era produced eight Hall of Famers.

Turning players into Hall of Famers is alchemy.

When Lombardi joined the franchise, he saw the team sitting comfortably on the cliff. Shackled with complacency. He knew they could do a lot better than that. He knew there was the gold of greatness lying within each of them. He just needed to unveil it.

He knew they had wings. He knew they could fly.

So, he pushed them off the cliff.

The cliff of complacency.

And they flew.

There is a Lombardi in each of us. We, too, can turn our employees into Hall of Famers.

How comfortable are you jumping off the cliff yourself? How comfortable are you unveiling your own greatness?

What do you see in your employees? Who they are or who they can be? The present or the potential?

Do you believe they have wings?

Do you believe they can fly?

Do you have the courage to push them off the cliff?

5. <u>Give credit, take the blame</u>

We are resilient.

We can put up with many quirks in our boss.

Demanding? Mercurial? Disciplinarian? Workaholic? Perfectionist?

No problem.

We find a way to thrive despite these quirks in a boss.

But the one quirk that we can't stand is when the boss takes credit for every success and blames us for every failure. It demoralizes us more than anything else.

The effect is the opposite of alchemy.

Instead of transforming good into great, good shrivels into "barely there."

Why put our heart and soul into something if we won't be recognized for our efforts? Why stick our neck out if we will be blamed for failure?

So, we drag our bodies to work. We clock in. And eagerly wait for 5 pm.

We are *barely there*.

John Wooden — the legendary head coach of the UCLA basketball team — knew he wouldn't be able to win championships if his players and coaches were dragging their bodies to the game. If their heads and hearts weren't fully in the game.

He understood the importance of leaders shielding their people from blame for failures and giving them credit for success.

In his book, *A Game Plan for Life: The Power of Mentoring*, he wrote, "If one of my assistant coaches made a suggestion that we decided to implement, I would make sure to praise him for his foresight in the press conference afterward. But if one made a suggestion that didn't prove to be as successful, I accepted the blame myself rather than pinning it on the assistant."[10]

Kareem Abdul Jabbar played three seasons with Wooden and won three NCAA championships. He remembered his former coach, "We understood that if we played up to the standard he had set in practice, we'd probably win. If not, if we lost, he took the blame and tried to fix it in the next practice."[11]

His players and coaches feared him.

But more importantly, they trusted him.

They knew he had their backs. They knew if they stuck their neck out by trying new things and failed, he would cover for them.

They also knew he wouldn't hog all the limelight. They knew he would shine the spotlight on them for the team's success.

Wooden led his team to 10 NCAA championships. More than any other head coach.

Wooden was an alchemist.

No wonder he was fondly called the "Wizard of Westwood."

Are you a "Me" person or "We" person?

When you are working on a project, do you care who gets the credit?

Are you comfortable sharing the credit for success with others?

Are you comfortable failing?

Are you comfortable with your team failing?

Are you comfortable taking the blame for your team's failure?

Does your team trust you?

Do they think you have their backs?

Would they fearlessly follow you?

Böttger, our alchemist from the beginning of the chapter, fearlessly followed his passion.

Did he ever get out that dungeon? Did he ever regain his freedom?

Yes. He did.

After he helped another scientist invent the process to make the white gold — the European porcelain.

Böttger was looking for yellow gold. Instead, he found white gold.

Columbus was looking for India. Instead, he found America.

Alchemy is not about arriving at your destination.

It's about leaving the status quo.

It's about embarking on a journey.

A journey of growth and transformation.

CHAPTER 7

THE FUTURE IS TURBULENT: BE A CAPTAIN

> *"Everybody's got a plan until they get hit."*
> Mike Tyson

"She has nerves of steel. That lady, I applaud her. I am going to send her a Christmas card...with a gift certificate for getting me on the ground." said one passenger about Tammie Jo Shults, the captain of the Southwest flight 1380.[1]

A Christmas card and a gift certificate for the pilot?

We don't even acknowledge the cabin crew while disembarking because we are so busy looking at our phones, so what gives?

On that fateful day, the outpouring of love, admiration, and respect for Captain Shults was understandable. In fact, it was well deserved.

She had just saved 148 lives.

Minutes after the flight took off from LaGuardia airport and reached an altitude of 32,000 feet, its left engine failed. A part of the engine broke off, hit the fuselage, and shattered a window in the main cabin, causing rapid decompression.

The aircraft shook, vibrated, rapidly descended, and snapped into a roll. The broken engine and shattered window in the main cabin made the plane hard to maneuver, like removing power steering from your car (then dropping the vehicle off a cliff).

People heard the muffled bang and saw the engine debris scrapping by the plane. They started to panic, scream and cry. Some held hands and prayed. Others frantically made what they believed would be last calls or last text messages to their loved ones.

Amidst this chaos, there was one person who remained calm, collected, and composed.

Luckily, it was the captain.

Her calmness is present in the recording of her conversation with the air traffic controller.

A reporter from CNN said Shults was so calm in the recording that she sounded like she was ordering a deli sandwich. Her mother-in-law said it sounded as "if she and I were sitting here talking."

Once on the ground, Shults came to the main cabin to explain to the passengers what had happened.

The details didn't matter to these thankful passengers. They just wanted to hug her, applaud her, and profusely thank her.

She waved off the accolades, saying it's easier to be the pilot in such a situation than a passenger.

When I grow up, I want to be just like Captain Shults.

(Heck, when you grow up, you may want to be like Captain Shults too.)

Why?

Because it's good for your career.

Because the future is turbulent, and you want to be the captain and not the passenger.

If you want to differentiate yourselves from the others, learn to display grace under fire. Learn to be a rock when everything around you is on shaky ground. Learn to navigate through terrifying terrain.

And then walk off as if it was *no big deal*.

That's cool.

And you know what else is cool?

Receiving Christmas cards and gift certificates from people who were previously just strangers.

Fasten your seat belt. *Emotional* turbulence ahead.

Most of us don't have to land an aircraft after losing an engine. Most of us don't have to navigate a ship through a perfect storm.

The turbulence we encounter is invisible and insidious but equally traumatic.

We face the emotional turbulence. Our cracked window is anxiety. Our failed engine is worry. Our loss of compression is fear.

Triggered by an unpredictable crisis.

Triggered by the crippling chaos.

Triggered by the ambiguous present.

Triggered by the unknown future.

Often, we think that to set up our teams for success, we just need to equip them with the latest technology, spoil them with free chef-prepared meals, grant them the freedom and flexibility they want, and off they go.

But they need one more thing from us.

Assurance.

Assurance that they are in good hands.

Assurance that we won't put them in harm's way even if there were an unpredictable crisis.

Assurance that we will find clarity amidst ambiguity.

Assurance that we will find the light at the end of the tunnel called the unknown future.

If they see us as a rock they can rely on, they will be inspired and energized. If they don't believe we have what it takes, they will be dispirited and debilitated.

Cultivate nerves of steel

The game clock shows three seconds. The Chicago Bulls calls a time-out.

The Bulls are trailing the Cleveland Cavaliers by one point. With the best-of-five playoff series tied at two games each, these last three seconds of game five will decide who wins the series.[2]

The pressure is palpable. You can see it on the faces of the players, coaches, and fans.

As the game resumes, Michael Jordan is double-teamed by Craig Ehlo and Larry Nance. His Airness first moves to his right, then cuts left to create space from his defender. He receives the inbound pass from Brad Sellers. Drifting left, Jordan makes a jump shot at the foul line over the defending Ehlo as time expires.[3]

The rest is history.

The Bulls win 101-100.

Just another day at the office.

Michael Jordan. The Buzzer Beater.

We have seen the "steely stare" of Tiger Woods. We have marveled at how he approaches the 18th green when the game is on the line.

He ignores the crowd, ignores the media, ignores the pressure itself.

He knows he has a job to do, so he gets it done.

Then, he walks away with a jacket and a trophy.

Just another day in the office.

Tiger Woods. The Finisher.

Then there is Tom Brady. Time and again, he knows he is about to be pounced on by a linebacker. He doesn't fear getting hit, he doesn't hurry, he doesn't panic.

He keeps his calm, trusts his defenders to do their job, and runs the play.

Just another day in the office.

Tom Brady. The Closer.

How do they make it look so easy?

How do they buzzer beat while many others buckle?

How do they finish while many others flinch?

How do they close while many others choke?

How?

By cultivating the nerves of steel.

Michael Jordan summed it up in his interview with ESPN, "People didn't believe me when I told them I practiced harder than I played…that's where my comfort zone was created. By the time game came, all I had to do was to react to what my body was already accustomed to doing."[4]

Michael Phelps, the legendary swimmer with 23 Olympic Gold Medals, uses visualization to prepare for any potential crisis.

Before each race, he rehearses what he will do if something goes wrong. He asks himself, "If my swimsuit ripped or if my goggles broke, what would I do?"[5]

His coach Bob Bowman explains, "He has all of this in his database, so that when he swims the race he's already programmed his nervous system to do one of those. And he'll just pick the one that happens to come up. If everything's perfect, he'll just go with the perfect one. If he has to make a change, he's got it in there."[6]

Do you think flight 1380 was the first rodeo for Captain Shults? Not at all.

Before joining Southwest Airlines, she was one of the first women pilots in the US Navy and the very first woman to fly F/A – 18

Hornet.[7] Being a woman, she had to try harder than her male counterparts. She had to prove she belonged in the cockpit.

When she was asked what specific experiences from her time with the US Navy helped her land flight 1380, she said, "The out-of-control flight (OCF) training. I ended up teaching OCF training for a year."

Think about it. She has been training other pilots how to control an "out-of-control" aircraft for a year. No wonder she sounded like she was ordering a deli sandwich. For her, it was just another day at the office.

What's the common thread across these examples?

They didn't bring nerves of jelly to the job and then, on a dime, channel superpowers to save the day.

They have been cultivating nerves of steel *for years*.

They have been preparing and practicing for a crisis *for years*.

They have been visualizing moments when an arena can turn into a pressure cooker *for years*.

They have been visualizing what to do when something goes wrong with a flight *for years*.

No superpowers. No luck. No god-given gift.

Just visualization. Preparation. Practice. Lots of it.

You can do it too.

Think about your job.

What could throw you off your game?

What stressful scenario would turn your office into a pressure cooker?

How would you handle any natural disaster impacting you and your team?

How would you handle a young and feisty competitor eating your lunch?

How would you handle losing a large client?

US President Grover Cleveland once said, "In calm waters, every ship has a good captain."

It's the turbulence that reveals the great ones.

That's why Jordan doesn't run away from the turbulence. He embraces it. Because for him, turbulence means an opportunity to shine — an opportunity to show the world what he is made of.

If you want to shine in your career, if you want to stand out among your peers, if you want to prove to your bosses that you are ready for the big league, then learn to embrace the turbulence.

Learn to cultivate the nerves of steel.

Visualize and practice being the oasis of calm amidst the chaos.

Visualize and practice being cool and yet in complete control.

Visualize and practice being the rock people can rely on.

Seek clarity amidst ambiguity

With 2020 came Covid19.

And suddenly, our world became ambiguous. Foggy. Confusing.

More and more questions. Fewer and fewer answers.

How does it spread? How long would it last? What precautions do we need to take? Are masks effective? How long would the lockdowns last? How long would we need to work from home? Would life ever be back to normal as we knew it? Would there be a new normal? What would that new normal look like? Would our employers survive this crisis? Would our businesses survive this crisis? What do we do with our employees, our customers, our investors, our communities?

No one had a crystal ball.

As I write this chapter in August of 2020, many of these questions still remain unanswered.

Not even a hint of light at the end of the tunnel.

"Can this year end any sooner? Can we get a vaccine and skip to 2021?"

People are getting tired. Too much confusion. Too much ambiguity.

Amidst this cacophony of confusion, a few have looked for clarity.

And they have found it.

Take small business owners Ryan Ruelos and Jon Poteet.

In July of 2019, they launched Shine Distillery and Grill in Portland, Oregon.[8] They had big plans for their 7000 square foot building with a 250-seat restaurant.

Those plans went out the door the moment they got hit.

Thanks to Covid19, their world — just like everyone else's — turned upside down.

But they didn't give in.

They looked for a path forward.

And found it.

They realized there was a shortage of hand sanitizers. They repurposed their distillery and put it to work. In just a couple of days, they were making, packaging, and offering these hand sanitizers to their patrons.

The word got out in the community, and people started flooding the restaurant. They would come into the store to buy a bottle of hand sanitizer and leave with a bottle of bourbon.

Their brand recognition went through the roof.

From "Shine who?" to "Shine everywhere."

What's their advice to other brick-and-mortar owners?

"Don't just make the most of what you have. Make something *new* with your infrastructure."

Talk about clarity amidst ambiguity.

Ruelos and Poteet are not alone.

Christina Karin, a Chicago based womenswear designer, launched the hashtag #maskchallenge and committed her own resources to make 10,000 masks for the front-liners.[9]

&Pizza offered free pizza to its employees and their immediate families and to healthcare workers. The company also increased its hourly pay by $1.[10]

U-Haul offered 30-day free self-storage to all college students who had been impacted by schedule changes at their universities.[11]

Often, when we come across an ambiguous situation, we think we don't know anything.

We feel everything is a question mark.

But is it?

We still know our Vision Mission Values. Ambiguity doesn't have to change that.

We still know our Purpose. Ambiguity doesn't have to change that.

If we have been saying, "Employees are the most important asset of our company" for years, why would ambiguity change that?

If we have been saying, "Customers are at the center of every decision we make" for years, why would ambiguity change that?

If we have been saying, "We believe in giving back to the community" for years, why would ambiguity change that?

Shine Distillery, Christina Karin, &Pizza and U-Haul didn't let ambiguity change their core beliefs. They didn't let the ambiguity derail them from their employee-centric, customer-centric, and community-centric philosophy.

Instead of cowering down to Covid19, they doubled down on what they stood for.

How do you find clarity amidst the ambiguity?

1. <u>Play a long game</u>

Instead of playing a short game, acting out of fear, these companies played a long game, acting out of courage. And in the process, they built a stronger brand — the one employees, customers, and communities are proud to be associated with.

One day, Covid19 shall pass. Once it does, the companies that played the long game, the companies that stayed true to their values, will reap the benefits.

Everything being equal, from where do you think people would prefer to buy their next bottle of bourbon or next box of pizza or next outfit? When these students grow up and move again, which moving and storage company do you think they would gravitate toward?

When you face an ambiguous situation, where you think you don't know anything, take a step back. List down everything you do know.

Your VMV. Your purpose. Your core beliefs and principles.

They are the powerful headlights that can pierce through the fog and let you find a path forward.

One way to play a long game is to imagine that you are looking back at the current crisis five or ten years from now. Ask yourself, would you be proud of the decisions you are making right now five or ten years from now? Looking back, would you feel you stayed true to your core values and beliefs, or would you feel you sold your soul?

Pondering and answering these questions will align you to your true north.

2. <u>Focus on the solution, not the problem</u>

When faced with an unpredictable crisis, it's easy to be overwhelmed. It's easy to focus on the problems you are facing. It's easy to focus on everything that's going wrong.

Tony Robbins famously said, "Wherever our attention goes, energy flows."

The more we dwell on the negative, the more energy flows to the negative. Giving it a life of its own. It starts to impede our ability to think rationally and creatively. It starts to engulf us with a sense of despair and hopelessness.

And then we give in.

Imagine if Captain Shults just focused her attention on a broken engine and a broken window. Imagine If she kept wondering what if the left engine continues to disintegrate, what if the wing gets damaged, what if the other engine caves in too.

All of these thoughts probably crossed her mind. But she stayed focused on the solution.

She communicated with air traffic control to find the nearest airport to attempt a landing. She chose the right runway and the right approach. She asked passengers to stay calm, "we are not going down, we are landing." She asked for paramedics to be ready. She said her prayer and then landed.

3. <u>Delegate</u>

When faced with a crisis, you don't have time to do everything. You need to stay focused on the most crucial issue at hand and delegate the rest to the team.

Author Sheryl Sandberg calls this "ruthless prioritization."

When the engine broke, and the aircraft started descending rapidly, Captain Shults didn't start sifting through the manuals to look for the emergency procedure. She didn't rush to the main cabin to survey the damage. She didn't pace the aisle helping people prepare for the brace position.

She took control of the aircraft and stayed focused on flying and landing it safely.

She relied on her first officer to find out what was happening in the main cabin. She relied on him to go through the emergency checklist. She relied on her crew to prepare the cabin for a bumpy landing.

4. <u>Be resourceful</u>

Everybody approaches a crisis differently. Everybody has a unique vantage point. Your team members may know things you may not. They may have clarity that you may not.

Ask if they have any ideas or suggestions on how to navigate through a crisis.

People may not share their ideas and suggestions on their own, especially during the crisis. The stakes are high. They don't want to be blamed if something were to go wrong.

You have to create an environment where they know the buck stops with you. If something goes wrong, you will take the blame.

If they trust you, they will open up.

Guess who came up with the idea to make hand sanitizers at the Shine distillery?

Not the owners. But one of the distillers.

One day, Covid19 will go away. But the turbulence will not.

The rise of AI, digital generations, and freelancers is dramatically altering our lives both at work and at home. The slow and sluggish — people, companies, industries — are disappearing. The alert and agile — people, companies, industries — are dominating.

The speed with which we need to upskill and reskill is accelerating. The pace with which we need to find a new job, a new company, a new industry is quickening.

The world is increasingly becoming the very thing we don't like.

More volatile. More uncertain. More complex. More ambiguous.

It's overwhelming. It's stressful. It's nerve-wracking.

But if you have taken the time and initiative to cultivate nerves of steel, you will shine. If you have learned to find clarity amidst ambiguity, you will stand out. If you can see the order within chaos, you will excel.

When the team is trailing by a point, and there are only three seconds to go, if you say to your bosses, "I will take care of this," your career is futureproof.

When giant linebackers are ready to pounce on you and trounce you, if you say to your bosses "consider it done," your career is futureproof.

When an engine fails, and the aircraft is severely damaged, if you say to your bosses, "I got this," your career is futureproof.

After 22 minutes of a harrowing ordeal, when flight 1380 finally landed and came to a halt, paramedics were waiting.

One of them checked Captain Shults' blood pressure.[12]

It was normal.

CHAPTER 8

THE FUTURE IS UNKNOWN: BE A FUTURIST

> *"I skate to where the puck is going, not where it's been."*
> Wayne Gretzky

Do you remember when VHS ruled the world?

There were only 23,500 websites (compared to over 1.74 billion in 2020).[1]

There was no Hotmail, much less Gmail.

And no Tickle Me Elmo.

The year was 1995.

The Internet was still in its nascent stage — slowly starting to gain popularity.

Two people were keenly following how this new phenomenon would shape our future. Ironically, they arrived at two completely different conclusions.

In February of 1995, Clifford Stoll, an astronomer and an author, wrote an article titled "The Internet? Bah!" in *Newsweek* magazine.[2]

In the tirade against the net, he wrote, "Visionaries see a future of telecommuting workers, interactive libraries, multimedia classrooms. They speak of electronic town hall meetings and virtual communities. Commerce and business will shift from offices and malls to networks and modems…Baloney."

He continued his rant, "Then there's cyber business. We're promised instant catalog shopping — just point and click for great deals. We'll order airline tickets over the Internet, make restaurant reservations, and negotiate sales contracts. Stores will become obsolete. So, how come my local mall does more business in an afternoon than the entire Internet handles in a month?"

Stoll predicted the Internet was a fad and would soon disappear (it might surprise you, but he was wildly wrong in his prediction).

Bill Gates, on the other hand, arrived at a different conclusion.

Three months after Stoll published the article, Gates sent out a 9-page memo titled "The Internet Tidal Wave" to Microsoft executives. He wanted to make sure his team was not ignoring or downplaying the Internet.[3]

He outlined the state of this new technology back then and where it was heading. He forewarned his team about the changing competitive landscape. He detailed the next steps his team needed to take to thrive amidst a disruptive future ahead.

He wrote, "I want to make clear that our focus on the Internet is crucial to every part of our business. The Internet is the most important single development to come along since the IBM PC was introduced in 1981...The Internet is a tidal wave. It changes the rules. It's an incredible opportunity as well as incredible challenge."

How did Stoll and Gates arrive at two different conclusions? Why did Stoll abandon the rink just as Gates started to lace up his skates?

Stoll was focused on *where the puck was*. Gates was focused on *where the puck was going*.

For Stoll, the puck was in a local mall doing brisk business (why would people buy anything from the Internet when they can easily go to a local mall?).

The puck was in bulky laptops (how would people carry them to the beach to read a book or a newspaper?).

The puck was in human touch (how could eCommerce thrive without the salespeople?).

For him, the future was *the present frozen in time*.

For Gates, the future was *brewing with possibilities arising from the present*.

For him, the puck was not stuck but moving.

And many of the possibilities he laid out in the memo became our reality over the last 25 years.

Time and again, he has been right about what the future had in store for us.

In a 2015 TED talk, the Microsoft Co-founder presciently predicted, "If anything kills over 10 million people in the next few decades, it's most likely to be highly infectious virus rather than a war. Not missiles, but microbes."[4]

Eerie, right?

How does he always know where the puck is going?

Does he have a better gut feeling or hunch or instinct than the rest of us?

Is he a psychic? Is he a clairvoyant?

Is there a room in his Seattle mansion with a crystal ball, tarot cards, or perhaps a Ouija board?

No.

He is merely a futurist.

He sees the approaching tidal wave.

Why?

Because his head is not buried in the sand.

Because he is looking at what's brewing on the horizon.

Don't project present to the future

Let the following predictions sink in for a second.

"The Americans have need for the telephone, but we do not. We have plenty of messenger boys." — Sir William Preece, The Chief Engineer, The British Post Office, 1878

"The horse is here to stay, but the automobile is only a novelty, a fad." — The president of the Michigan Savings Bank, advising Henry Ford's lawyer not to invest in the Ford Motor Company in 1903

"Television won't be able to hold on to any market it captures after the first six months. People will soon get tired of staring at a plywood box every night." — Darryl Zanuck, 20th Century Fox, 1946

In the examples above, three different people making three different predictions about three different products at three different times.

But they have one thing in common.

They were all wrong because they projected their present to the future.

There are plenty of messenger boys. Why would people want telephones?

Horses have been reliable for centuries. Why would people buy automobiles?

Life is good with radio. Why would people want TV?

If people are happy with life as is, why would they need or want anything new?

Just because we are happy with the present, just because we are happy with life as is, doesn't mean the future will stop *futuring*.

No matter how much we love our present, no matter how much we want to hold on to the present, the future will continue to unfold.

The present will never become the future.

So why project it onto the future?

Instead, do what Gates does.

1. Be curious.
2. Study and synthesize.
3. Extrapolate.

Curious how to "be like Bill?" Good. That's a start.

Be curious

Don't get me wrong, I love my daughter Clara.

But she is starting to get on my nerves.

A fellow parent shared a depressing statistic with me: "a four-year-old girl typically asks 390 questions a day".

Clara isn't even four yet, but it feels like she averages well over 400 questions per day.

From the moment she wakes up to the moment she falls asleep, she keeps firing away a barrage of questions.

Question 1: "Why is the sky blue?"
Question 2: "Why can't I eat soap?"
Question 3: "What are the stars made off?"
Question 4: "Why can't I stay up as late as you?"
Question 5: "Are we rich?" (well, if you let me finish this book…)

For her, the world is a fascinating place. Everything is new. There is just so much to learn, see, and do.

When something catches her attention, she wants to know more about it.

The other day, around question #139, she asked, "Dad, what are these ants doing?"

Since my response was somewhat of an eye-roll, she took the matter into her own hands. She lay on her belly, brought her face close to the floor, and watched ants do what ants do — for an hour!

She is not alone. All kids her age know they will only learn if they are curious and if they ask questions.

But as adults, we stop asking questions and stop being curious because we live with a paradox of our own making.

If kids ask questions, we consider them smart and intelligent. But if adults ask questions, we consider them dim and dense.

To be a futurist, we must reclaim our childlike curiosity. We must look at the world with the same sense of wonder as a four-year-old.

As the science fiction writer William Gibson said, "Future is already here. It's just unevenly distributed."

We are surrounded by clues as to how the future may unfold. We just have to be aware of them. We have to observe the puzzle pieces around us. We have to pay attention to what is, but also what could be.

Does Alexa respond to you in a happy or sad tone based on how you feel? That's a clue.

Are your kids learning new skills watching YouTube videos? That's a clue.

Are *you* learning new skills watching a YouTube video? That's even a *bigger* clue.

Is your company implementing a flexible work-from-home policy? That's a clue.

Did you read a news article about Hyundai making flying cars for Uber? That's a clue.

Did your friend leave her job to become a freelancer? That's a clue.

Do your kids have so little patience they can't even sit through a 15-second TikTok video? That's a clue.

If this were a murder case, the future would be in cuffs by now. There are clues everywhere!

We are all exposed to the same clues.

How does a non-futurist differ from a futurist?

A non-futurist will move on to the next distraction, next thought, next trending headline, next app. Scroll up. Scroll down. Scroll left. Scroll right. Miss everything.

Futurists, on the other hand, get down on the ground to see what the ants are doing. They stop, they zoom in, they pay attention.

They study. They synthesize.

Study and Synthesize

In 1999, Steven Spielberg invited fifteen experts to a hotel in Santa Monica for a three-day "think tank summit."[5] The attendees came from all walks of life. A philosopher, an architect, a journalist, an author, a computer scientist, a biomedical researcher, an artist, among others.

What was Spielberg up to?

He was working on his next movie, Minority Report, which was to be set in the year 2054. He wanted the future depicted in the movie to be well studied and well synthesized.

After three days, the summit produced an 80-page document labeled "2054 Bible."

John Underkoffler, a researcher at MIT's prestigious media lab, was one of the participants.

He reminisced about working on the document:

"It covered everything from architectural overviews, the trends that led to more vertical buildings and cities…the political tenor of the times, the individual economics of different strata that led to certain architectural forms, right on down to the gadgets — the nonlethal weapons, the hover packs, the little spider robots that run around and identify you. For everything you see on the screen, there's actually a hundred times more well-knit back story."[6]

Well-knit back story.

How well-knit is your back story?

It's not just a movie, it's your life.

Are you reacting or acting?

Are you reacting to the future as it unfolds?

Or

Are you acting based on the back story you have put together?

Are you taking the time to study the clues and trends? Are you synthesizing these clues and trends?

Studying a clue or a trend in isolation is easy.

But trends don't manifest in isolation. They merge, they intersect, they intermingle. And often, they sprout from each other.

Synthesizing them across various disciplines — such as technology, environment, politics, economics — is hard but critically important.

Let's look at a more specific example.

One of the trends that may emerge from the Covid-19 crisis is the popularity and practicality of the work-from-home model. If there is one thing this crisis has taught us is that we don't need to be present in person all the time. With the latest enabling technology, we can be equally effective working remotely.

It's highly likely that, even after the crisis, companies and employees may continue to embrace this flexible work arrangement.

If that happens, companies may not need as much office space as before. How does this intersect with other trends in the commercial real estate market?

If the employees have the freedom to work from home, would they consider moving out of expensive and congested big cities? How would this intersect with trends in the residential real estate market?

How would this shift impact local economies?

As people move from big cities (traditionally progressive) to smaller cities (traditionally conservative), how does this change the political landscape? How would it intersect with other political undercurrents?

How would this impact the freelancing trend? People flock to freelancing for the freedom to work from wherever, whenever, however. What if companies start offering the same freedom to their full-time employees?

The broader and deeper your synthesis, the richer your back story (aka the better your movie).

Your back story doesn't need to be about 2054.

Start with the next 10 years.

Your back story doesn't need to be about changing the world.

Start with staying relevant in your job.

Ask yourself, how will the rise of AI, digital generations, and freelancers at the workplace impact your career in the next 10 years?

You don't have to host fifteen experts in a five-star resort for a three-day "think tank summit."

We live in a golden age of information.

For every trend or clue that intrigues you, there are books, blogs, websites, and podcasts.

Everything you want to know is at your fingertips if you know where to look.

Study. Synthesize.

And then extrapolate.

Extrapolate

"Floyd sometimes wondered if the Newspad, and the fantastic technology behind it, was the last word in man's quest for perfect communications. Here he was, far out in the space, speeding away from Earth at thousands of miles an hour, yet in milliseconds he could see the headlines of any newspaper he pleased."[7]

We can all relate to this narrative now in 2020.

But this was written in 1968. Sir Arthur C Clarke envisioned an electronic "Newspad" in his famous novel *2001 A Space Odyssey*.

His vision came to life 42 years later when Apple introduced the iPad in 2010.

Clarke is not alone when it comes to envisioning the future.

In 1909, when landlines were still a novelty, Nikola Tesla predicted that one day, we would all be walking around with phones in our pockets.[8]

In 1865, when horses were still the primary mode of transportation, Jules Verne authored a book *From the Earth to the Moon* and predicted the moon landing.[9]

How do these futurists do it?

In hindsight, it seems so magical.

But, it's not.

It is methodical.

There is a method to their magic.

Futurists study current trends, the direction of these trends, the velocity of these trends, the interplay of these trends. And then they extrapolate these findings to the future.

You can do it too

Think about the velocity, direction, and interplay of AI, digital generations, and freelancers (and other trends) impacting your career.

When you extrapolate your findings 10 years from now, what do you envision?

Will you still be doing what you are doing now?

Will your job description change? If so, how?

Do you envision working from home or in the office?

Do you see yourself as a freelancer or a full-time employee?

What technology will you be "partnering with?"

What skills will you be using that you are not using today?

Will you need to change your job or company or industry because they may be obsolete?

If there are changes, what do you see yourself doing?

As you reflect on these questions, you gain more clarity about your life 10 years down the road. You gain more clarity about the skills gap you will need to fill to be relevant. You gain more clarity about initiating the right changes in your life. Starting now.

Time to update our LinkedIn profile

It's time to update our LinkedIn profile and give ourselves a new title: a futurist.

We can't afford to be just a doctor or an engineer or a marketing executive. We need to be a *futurist* and doctor, *futurist* and engineer, *futurist* and marketing executive.

We are not talking about *leaving our day jobs* to become a professional futurist.

We are talking about *keeping our day jobs* for the next 10 years.

We invest so much of our time in reading books and blogs, watching videos and listening to podcasts, attending conferences and seminars.

Why?

So that we can become better at what we are doing today. A better salesperson, a better lawyer, a better HR professional.

But what if the job we trying to become better at doesn't exist in 10 years?

Imagine you trying to be the best horse cart driver in 1900 and then being jobless in 1910.

Let's not put the cart before the horse.

Let's master the art of being a futurist first. Let's learn everything we can about the automobiles and anticipate its potential impact on our careers and our lives over the next ten years.

Let's learn to be like Wayne Gretzky.

When Wayne Gretzky entered the NHL in 1979, critics wrote him off: "He is too small, too wiry, and too slow to be a force in NHL."[10]

That year, Gretzky tied for first place in scoring and was named the Most Valuable Player.

Over the next 20 years, he became the leading scorer in NHL history, with more goals and assists than any other player. He was named the Most Valuable Player nine times. He is considered the greatest hockey player by his fans, his critics, and the league itself.

His nickname? "The great one."

Not the biggest. Not the fastest.

But the very best at one thing.

Anticipating. Always knowing where the puck was going.

Do you know where your puck is going?

Where will it be in 10 years?

SECTION III

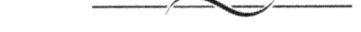

FUTUREPROOF YOUR COMPANY

In this section, you will learn how to:

- Transform your business digitally to stay relevant
- Infuse purpose that guides your company as the true north
- Unleash the spirit of innovation to be a disruptor
- Inspire learning to groom the workforce of tomorrow
- Enjoy expedition by engaging your employees

CHAPTER 9

THE FUTURE IS DIGITAL: TRANSFORM BUSINESS

> *"Citizens are speaking to their governments using 21st century technologies, governments are listening on 20th century technology and providing 19th century solutions."*
> Madeleine Albright, US Secretary of State

"It was big and clunky," you might say. "About the size of a toaster."

It weighed 8 pounds and required 16 AA batteries. It took 23 seconds to take and store a black and white photograph with a resolution of 0.01MP. It was the world's first portable digital camera, and only one person saw its potential.[1]

The year was 1975. A 24-year-old engineer turned inventor named Steven Sasson excitedly shared the news about his latest invention. His bosses at Eastman Kodak were unimpressed.

According to Sasson, their reaction was, "Print had been with us for over 100 years, no one was complaining about the prints, they were very inexpensive, and so why would anyone want to look at their picture on a television set?"[2]

Kodak filed for bankruptcy in 2012.[3]

Secretary Albright was referring to the public sector when she raised the alarm about the dire need for digital transformation. If she was also referring to the private sector, she would have been spot-on.

Why digital transformation?

We covered three disruptive forces in the first section of the book: AI, digital generations, and the gig economy.

As these swelling forces gain momentum over the next decade, they have the potential to significantly disrupt the ecosystem you operate in. They have the potential to radically change what customers and employees expect of you. And hence, if you don't transform, they have the potential to render your very business model obsolete.

While, out of habit, you may be busy training your guns on an age-old rival in your industry, these forces furnish a fertile ground for a disruptor (like Amazon for retail, Airbnb for hospitality, and Uber for transportation) to sprout out of nowhere to out-wit, out-think, and outmaneuver you and eat your lunch forever.

Speaking of lunch, take Domino's Pizza as an example.

During the last decade, the company has taken a big slice of market share from its competitors — Pizza Hut and Papa John's.

How did the 60-year company pull this off?

By reinventing itself as a young and feisty disruptor.

Just 12 years ago, Domino's Pizza was struggling in the marketplace. Sales and the stock price were falling. Customers complained the crust tasted like cardboard and the pizza sauce tasted like ketchup.[4]

So, it revamped its recipe. It created a richer, spicier sauce, tastier cheese combination, and a buttery crust with garlic and herbs.

Revamping the recipe was a no-brainer.

But Domino's brilliantly revamped one more thing.

The company's business model.

It aspired to become an eCommerce company that sells pizza. It crafted, invested in, and implemented an ambitious digital transformation strategy.

Remember the days when you could order Domino's Pizza only two ways — by walking into a restaurant or by calling?

Today, Domino's offers 15 different ways to order pizza.[5]

You can simply go to an app and order the pizza.

You don't like clicking through the app. No problem. There is a Zero Click option.

You like emojis more than words. No problem. Just text a pizza emoji.

You don't like words or emojis. No problem. Just talk to Google Home or Alexa.

The company wants to make ordering pizza as "frictionless as possible."

The ordering process is just one part of the company's multi-pronged digital strategy. It is also innovating ways to make pizza delivery faster, smarter, and hassle-free.

In 2016, it became the first company to deliver the world's first-ever pizza by drone.[6] And now, it's actively studying and trying out ways to deliver pizza through autonomous vehicles.

(Don't know how much to tip the pizza delivery person? Well, pretty soon, that's one less thing you may need to use your brain cells for.)

Thanks to its ambitious digital transformation, Domino's has not only regained its footing over the last decade but also significantly increased its market share. In February 2020, Domino's earned a 50 percent share of online spend in the pizza delivery market against Pizza Hut's 29 percent and Papa Johns' 21 percent.[7]

Whether your company is making pizza or Porsche, designing and executing a digital transformation strategy is no longer just nice-to-do. It's a must-do.

You must craft and implement a strategy that creates *value* for your key stakeholders and ensures you thrive in the marketplace.

A strategy that outlines how your business can leverage the latest technologies to personalize and harmonize your customer experience through all customer touchpoints; to make the customer experience better, faster, and smarter; to satisfy the emergent "on-demand" culture.

A strategy that outlines how, when, and where to deploy the latest technologies to replace or augment your employees; how to upgrade your technology to meet the demands of digital generations storming the workplace; how to deploy the right tools to promote better cohesion, communication, and cooperation within the distributed workforce of the future.

A strategy that outlines if there is a need for completely revamping the business model. And if so, how to go about it.

Easier said than done?

Indeed.

According to a McKinsey study in 2018, only 16 percent of the respondents say their organizations' digital transformations have successfully improved performance and also equipped them to sustain changes.[8]

Why do most digital transformations fail?

Companies often fail in their efforts because they believe digital transformation is all about the technology.

"If only we had the right technology in place, business problems would be solved."

It's tempting to think that technology is the elixir that will heal your bottom line by eradicating inefficiencies plaguing your company.

It's tempting to think that technology is the alchemist that will jumpstart your topline growth by transforming everything it touches (like your employees and customers) into gold.

It's tempting to think that if you buy and deploy the latest technology, you are futureproof.

Buying technology before defining the business strategy is not only putting the cart before the horse, but it's taking this mismatched carriage onto the highway.

Four "C"s of successful digital transformation

To orchestrate and execute a successful digital transformation that meets its objectives, we have to also focus on the 4 "C"s: CEO, Clarity, Coordination, and Caution.

<u>CEO</u>:

The buck stops with the CEO.

And hence, it should also begin with them.

The CEO should be the one crafting and championing the digital transformation strategy (yes, you read it right: CEO, not the CIO).

We are used to the CIO taking the lead on projects requiring investments in both technologies and IT resources. Usually, the CEO is kept updated with a quarterly progress report. This works for the projects that tinker with the back-end IT infrastructure with minimal, if any, impact to key stakeholders.

But the digital transformation is different. It not only transforms how key stakeholders (customers, employees, partners, investors) relate to technology but also (and more importantly) with each other.

Its reach is limitless with the potential to encompass all departments and all stakeholders (both internal and external).

It brings leaders face to face with the moment of truth. Face to face with the most fundamental and existential (and often the most difficult) questions about the company such as…

Why do we exist today?

What's our value proposition today?

Why should we exist in the future?

What should be our value proposition in the future?

How can we continue to exist (and thrive) in the future?

Think about it.

Only the CEO (not the CIO) owns the accountability for answering (and revisiting and rethinking and then answering again) these fundamental questions. *And getting it right.*

Only the CEO (not the CIO) has the authority and oversight to rally the troops across the entire organization and beyond.

The buck doesn't just start with the CEO. It needs to stay with the CEO.

It's not enough to invite the CEO to kick-start the project and rally the troops at a ceremonial ribbon cutting. They have to remain close to it until it's completed as if the company's life depends on it. Because most likely, it does.

Clarity:

Your employees need clarity about the "why."

Simon Sinek made the phrase "start with why" famous, but it's not just advice, it's a fundamental approach to business.

As you embark on this digital transformation journey, your employees may ask…

Why is the company investing so much time, effort, and money on this initiative?

Why is the company changing my job?

Why is the company changing my department?

Why is the company asking me to learn new skills?

Why is the company moving my cheese?

These are just some of the questions your employees may ask once the transformation is rolled out.

If leaders can eloquently articulate the "why" to stakeholders, the rest of the questions — what, when, who, and how — become easier to answer.

But before you, as leaders, can explain the "why" to stakeholders at large, you have to fully fathom the forces (both internal and external) impelling you to launch this important initiative.

This "why" is for you...

Why do you need to digitally transform?

What will happen if you don't?

How are your competitors transforming?

Is there a young and feisty "digital only" disruptor ready to pounce?

What happens if you don't enhance customer experience?

What happens if you don't enhance employee experience?

What happens if you don't change your business model?

Once you feel the gravity of these answers, once you start losing sleep over these answers, once you accept not just "why" but also "why now," you will gain clarity.

Clarity to stir the rest to action!

Coordination:

If an orchestra only features highly accomplished musicians, why do they need a conductor?

Because while musicians are busy playing their instruments to the best of their ability, it's the conductor who ensures there is harmony and synchrony among them. It's the conductor who ensures what we hear is symphony, not cacophony.

Just because the CEO is championing the initiative (with a clearly defined "why") and just because they have assigned the top 100 performers from across the organization to be a part of the initiative, it doesn't mean the end result will be beautiful music.

Lack of coordination (among even the best performers) can easily result in chaos and commotion. Have you ever heard the expression, "A camel is a horse designed by a committee?"

In any business transformation undertaking, there are a lot of moving pieces involving a lot of different people from a lot of different departments, with a lot of different agendas.

And what makes it even more challenging is that usually, none of these people are fully dedicated to the undertaking. They have day jobs. They have their own musical instruments to play.

That's why you need conductors. The ones who are not busy playing any instruments. The ones who don't have day jobs. The ones whose only job is to ensure that the people assigned to the project are working in harmony, working in coordination with others to achieve key milestones.

Companies need this coordination at both C-level (where the strategy and resource allocations are defined) and at the rank and file level (where most of the work gets done).

At C-level, one of the best practices is to bring onboard a dedicated senior executive, typically a Chief Digital Officer (CDO). Someone with a keen understanding of how the latest digital technologies can help companies achieve business goals. Someone with experience in successfully implementing similar initiatives.

According to a McKinsey study, companies who bring onboard a dedicated CDO are 1.6 times more likely to succeed. This makes sense because the CDO plays a critical role in ensuring the entire C-Suite remains fully informed, engaged, and aligned throughout the project's duration. And if the C-suite is aligned, they can get their respective troops to fall in line as well.

The CDO's experience also comes handy in coordinating the talent required for this undertaking and conducting the crucial talent gap analysis. Does the company have the right "digital" talent internally? Does it need to hire externally? Are there internal candidates willing and ready to be upskilled?

While the coordination at the organization's highest levels is critical, it is equally important to have a dedicated project management team that synchronizes the efforts across the organization with the rank and file employees.

This team makes sure everyone is doing their part in harmony, meeting deadlines, and escalating issues if they arise.

This team plays a crucial role in conducting the orchestra.

Symphony. Not cacophony.

<u>Cautious</u>:

"Don't bite off more than you can chew," was a common expression in our household, not only around the dinner table, but when we tried to tackle hefty goals.

Clichés are clichés for a reason. They're timeless bits of wisdom.

This expression is also highly relevant today, whether you are taking a bite of a triple-decker burger or launching a digital transformation project.

You are hungry. You are excited. You don't have much time.

So, you go in with all guns blazing. Trying to digitally transform your organization. All at once.

As fast as you can. But the faster you go, the slower the transformation seems to take place.

Why? For three reasons...

Because your company's inherent inertia hasn't caught up with your excitement (yet).

Because your employees haven't started drinking by the fire hose like you have (yet).

Because you haven't built up any momentum by earning small wins (yet).

Sure, you realize you are investing a lot of time, effort, and money. But the ROI is missing.

Hopefully, sooner rather than later, you realize you bit off more than you can chew.

Digital transformation is a multi-year marathon rather than a short sprint. The slower, more methodical, more cautious you are (especially in the beginning), the faster you achieve your goal.

It sounds counterintuitive.

It sounds like advice you hear from a traditional, outdated, and out-of-touch company.

But this is the approach used by the most agile and nimble among us: the startups.

Instead of going all in, all guns blazing all at once, they like to break the marathon into short sprints, into smaller milestones, all leading to the ultimate end goal.

They focus on achieving each of these smaller "bite-size" milestones one after the other. Gathering data at the end of each sprint, taking note of the learnings, and applying them to the next sprint.

They build momentum. One sprint at a time. Then, the employees start to pay attention.

They witness the sprints. They witness the milestones. They witness the traction. They witness the progress.

More importantly, they witness the impact of digital transformation in their own jobs.

It's not a PowerPoint slide anymore. It's real. Something they can touch and feel.

Now they are energized, excited, and engaged.

Now, they're not only ready for the next bite, but their next meal, and no one is going to eat their lunch again.

CHAPTER 10

THE FUTURE IS MEANINGFUL: INFUSE PURPOSE

> *"Find your own Calcutta."*
> Mother Teresa

The announcement was a shocker! People couldn't believe it.

Just days before Thanksgiving, Patagonia declared it would donate 100 percent of its global sales on Black Friday to grassroots organizations working to protect the environment for future generations.[1]

Why would any company pledge away sales generated on any day, let alone Black Friday? Why do this on a day when the holiday shopping frenzy officially kicks off? Why do this on one of the biggest shopping days of a year?

Just, why?

Because Patagonia had found its own Calcutta. Because Patagonia had found its purpose. Because Patagonia believes in "Protecting and preserving the environment for future generations."

When someone asked Mother Teresa how they could make a difference in the world, she famously said, "Find your own Calcutta...you can find Calcutta all over the world if you have eyes to see."[2]

When Smirnoff realized that the top ten most-streamed tracks on Spotify didn't feature any female artists, the top-selling Vodka brand partnered with the streaming company to launch an initiative called *Smirnoff Equalizer*.[3] It was designed to help listeners discover talented female artists and their phenomenal music.

Through this effort, Smirnoff increased streaming for female artists by 52 percent. It created 2.7 million opportunities for listeners to discover them.

Why did Smirnoff, *a maker of Vodka*, invest time, effort, money for this initiative?

Because it had found its own Calcutta. Because it had found its purpose. Because Smirnoff believes in "Promoting gender equality in the music industry."

CVS Pharmacy stopped selling cigarettes and tobacco products at more than 7,600 stores in the US (knowing full well it would lose roughly $2 billion in revenue).[4] Why? Because it had found its purpose. Because CVS believes in "Helping people achieve better health."

Timberland, a global outdoor lifestyle brand, announced a commitment to plant 50 million trees around the world in five years.[5] Why? Because it had found its purpose. Because it believes in "Creating a greener future for all."

The list goes on and on and on.

Why Infuse Purpose?

So, what's up with this bandwagon approach to purpose?

Why are companies willing to spend so much time, effort, and money for purpose?

Planting 50 million trees?

Spending millions of dollars?

Giving up billions of dollars in revenue?

Just for "Purpose." Seriously?

What happened to the good ole' days where companies wrote a paragraph about their philanthropy in an annual report and posted a photo of CEO giving away a giant check?

Well, those days are gone, just like the shoulder pads and three-button suits.

Writing an annual check to a beneficiary is out. Posing for fake pictures is out. Pretending to care is out. But paying daily with your blood, sweat, tears (and money) for your cause? That's in.

Passive philanthropy is out. Activist engagement is in.

A company guiding the philanthropy is out. Purpose guiding the company is in.

The world is evolving.

A generational shift is unfolding.

Millennials and Gen Zers are storming the global economy. They are becoming a dominant force in the marketplace, both as employees and as consumers.

And they are bringing along a heightened sense of urgency for solving the most difficult issues facing the world today.

And no, they are not content to be mere bystanders.

They are not content to passively watch NGOs and inter-governmental agencies tackle these issues.

They want to take the bull by the horns themselves and tame it. And until they are successful, they are bringing along this bull to your offices, to your shops, and to your online communities.

And when they visit you, they want to know that you are equally passionate about taking this bull by the horns and taming it (and if not, they might let it loose in your China shop!).

Your customers and employees are evolving

Your customers don't buy what you make. They buy what you stand for.

Your customers are not loyal to you because they believe in your products. They are loyal to you because they believe in what you believe in.

According to an Accenture study conducted in 2018, 64 percent of global consumers find brands that actively communicate their purpose more attractive.[6]

The number is even higher in the US.

According to a Cone/Porter Novelli 2019 study, 83 percent of US consumers are more likely to be loyal to brands that lead with purpose.[7]

And these customers are not just speaking out in these surveys and studies. They are also making their voices heard with their wallets.

According to Kantar Purpose 2020 study, purpose-driven brands grew their valuation by 175 percent over the previous 12 years, whereas companies without any purpose grew by just 70 percent.[8]

The purpose is equally important to your employees.

What inspires them is not just the money you put in their pockets but also the money you put where your values are.

What inspires them is not just landing a big job in your company but also lending a hand for a bigger cause championed by your company.

Think about it. If wages and salaries are enough for people, everyone at work should be fully engaged and fully satisfied.

That's not the case.

According to a Gallup study conducted in 2018, only 34 percent of US workers are engaged at their workplace. A majority of them, 53 percent, are not engaged, and the remaining 13 percent are actively disengaged.[9]

They are all getting paid, right? So, what gives?

People are looking for more than money.

They are looking for meaning.

They are looking for a workplace where they can make a difference. They are looking for a workplace where they can contribute toward a larger purpose.

And when they find it, they are no longer dragging their bodies to work every day.

They are inspired and ready to give you their blood, sweat, and tears!

And why is this important for the employers?

Research conducted by Bain and Company concluded that if a satisfied employee's productivity level is 100 percent, an engaged employee's level is 144 percent, but the productivity level of an employee that is truly inspired by the purpose of their employer is a whopping 225 percent.[10]

Imagine a company where every employee is inspired and giving 225 percent!

It's like doubling your workforce...

Imagine a company where every customer is a fiercely loyal brand-ambassador!

It's like quadrupling your salesforce...

For many companies, it's just that: Imagination or a utopian dream.

But a few (purpose-driven) companies strive to make it a reality.

They do so by defining their purpose, living and breathing their purpose, animating their purpose, and connecting employees to their purpose.

How to build a purpose-driven organization?

1. Define your purpose

Defining a company's purpose is like laying a building's foundation.

To get it right, you have to dig deeper.

To get it right, you have to ask the right question.

The question that drills through the surface of what you do, how you do it, who does it, and by when.

The question that stops you in your tracks.

The "why..."

Why do you exist?

Why do you do what you do?

The answer to this question is your purpose.

The other questions test your head. The "why" tests your heart.

The other questions are about how a company can benefit itself. The "why" is about how a company can benefit *others*.

Why does Zappos exist? To deliver happiness.

Why does Kellogg exist? To nourish families so they can flourish and thrive.

Why does Microsoft exist? To empower every person and every organization on the planet to achieve more.

Why does Tesla exist? To accelerate the world's transition to sustainable energy.

Why does JetBlue exist? To inspire humanity — both in the air and on the ground.

None of these companies said their purpose was to meet quarterly financial targets. Or to deliver shoes, to make cereal, software or cars, or to fly planes.

It's all about how they can benefit others. It's all about how they can bring happiness to others. Nourish others. Empower others. Take care of the environment for others. Inspire humanity for others...

So, how do you find your purpose?

Taking your C-suite to an offsite soiree won't cut it.

You have to go beyond the distant and often disconnected ivory tower.

You have to go where the rubber meets the road.

You have to go to your front-line employees, your customers, and your communities.

You have to conduct town hall meetings, focus groups, and one-on-ones.

Listen to people express and articulate how your products or services are impacting their lives.

If you ask the right questions and listen carefully, you will unearth some gold nuggets (delivering happiness, not shoes!).

Nuggets to craft your purpose.

Once you have a purpose statement, make sure it's inspiring and timeless.

Ask around. Is it authentic enough for your employees, customers, your communities to be inspired by it?

Is it timeless? Would your purpose be meaningful and relevant in 2120?

Your strategies, tactics, and products are like the stars, planets, and constellations. They move. They shift.

But your purpose is like the North Star. Steady. Stable.

You know where to look when you are lost and don't know where to go.

Should we give up billions of dollars in revenue from tobacco sales? Should we give up revenue from Black Friday?

Don't know what to do?

Just look for your True North.

2. Live and breathe your purpose

"Eat your vegetables, Clara!" I said to my three-year-old the other day. She ignored what I said. Instead, she looked at the untouched pile of vegetables on my plate.

Whether we are 3 or 103, we know hypocrisy the moment we see it.

Our actions speak louder than our words.

As leaders, if you want your employees to live and breathe your purpose, start with the mirror.

Are you living and breathing it?

Think about it. What is worse than not having a company purpose?

Having a company purpose and not following it. Nothing turns off people more than hypocrisy.

Once you pledge to live by a lofty ideal, you live in a fishbowl.

People watch your every move. Both in what you choose to do and what you choose not to do.

People listen to your every word. Both in what you choose to say and what you choose not to say.

If this is just a shrewd marketing gimmick or a splashy publicity stunt, they will see through it.

If the purpose is collecting dust on your office walls, on your coffee mugs, or in your PowerPoint presentations, they will make a note of it.

And once they do, good luck exhorting them to go the extra mile for the company!

But here is the good news. The opposite is equally true.

If they feel your sincerity and authenticity, if they see you walking your talk, if they see you making difficult decisions to stay aligned with your true north, then they will be inspired.

They will walk over hot coals for you.

They will start living and breathing the company's purpose.

They will start eating their vegetables.

(So, yes, I have started eating my vegetables. And while I am at it, I am also saying "Please" and "Thank you" more often! Who said living and breathing your purpose was easy!)

3. <u>Animate your purpose</u>

You have defined your purpose. People have bought into it.

Now what?

Time to bring it to life. Everyday. Everywhere. In Everything.

Let it animate how you recruit and retain people. How you make and sell products. How you make easy and (especially) difficult decisions. How you behave in good times and (especially) in bad times.

This often means dumping the culture and values that mean nothing to you (one of Enron's core value was Integrity after all).

Instead, embrace the culture and values aligned with your purpose. The ones that stir you to action.

How does Zappos deliver happiness? With happier employees. One of the values at the company is to "create fun and a little weirdness." Recruits are often asked, "on a scale of 1 to 10, how weird are you?"[11] (Yup, if you happen to live in Vegas and consider yourself a little weird, you've got a shot!)

How does Patagonia animate its purpose of protecting the environment?

By hand-picking the people who share the same passion for the environment and outdoors. And it doesn't stop there. On your first day, you are given a booklet titled "Let my people go surfing." It's literally the employee handbook.[12]

When the surf is up near the head office, employees can drop everything and go ride the waves (and they do). No questions asked.

You think that's crazy?

It gets crazier.

If you get arrested for peacefully protesting for the environment, the company will come to your rescue and post bail for you and your spouse.

May be hiring weirdos or bailing out your employees is not for you.

It doesn't need to be.

Create your own culture and values that align with your purpose.

Something original. Something unique. Something organic.

Something that will leap off your walls and animate your halls!

4. <u>Connect people to purpose</u>

"I combat terrorism," read one of the thousands of responses.

No, it was not written by a US marine but by an employee at KPMG, an *accounting* firm.

The company had launched a 10,000 stories challenge asking employees to connect the dots between what they do on a daily basis and how it made a difference in the world.[13]

Employees loved the challenge.

It compelled them to take a step back from a tree and look at the forest.

They realized they were a part of a larger purpose.

They realized they were making a difference.

They weren't just preventing money laundering but combating terrorism by keeping the financial resources out of the hands of terrorists.

They weren't just certifying results in South Africa's first democratic election, but championing democracy.

The more they connected the dots, the more they felt empowered and energized.

They sent in 42,000 stories (well above the goal of 10,000!).

Stories full of pride in what they do at KPMG.

The following year, the company surged 17 spots on Fortune's annual 100 best companies to work for list.[14]

KPMG is not alone.

How did JetBlue win the JD Power award for customer satisfaction in 2019?[15]

By connecting all employees (no matter what their job was) to its core purpose of inspiring humanity in the air and on the ground.

The company gave everybody the same title. Whether you are a janitor, call center agent, check-in agent, baggage handler, or a CEO, you are a "crewmember" of JetBlue.

Everyone knows they are as mission-critical to making air travel less stressful and more humane as the folks flying the planes.

So how do you connect your people to your purpose?

Help them see the big picture.

We all get sucked into living in a box.

We all get sucked into a routine.

Wake up. Go to work. Clock in. Do the mundane. Clock out. Go home.

Repeat.

A mind-numbing, soul-shrinking routine.

We all need a nudge to get out of this routine.

We all need a push to get out of the box.

To notice how what we do in our little box impacts the big world outside.

Once we do, the light bulbs go off!

We find our Calcutta.

Suddenly...

Crunching numbers turns into combating terrorism.

Handling baggage turns into inspiring humanity.

Shipping boxes turns into delivering happiness.

Laying bricks turns into building a cathedral.

The mundane morphs into magical.

CHAPTER 11

THE FUTURE IS BOUNDLESS: UNLEASH INNOVATION

> *"If you want to build a ship, don't drum up people to gather wood, divide the work, and give orders. Instead, teach them to yearn for the vast and endless sea."*
> Antoine de Saint-Exupery

Arthur Fry had had enough! He had dropped his last piece of paper. He had lost the last page in his book.[1]

As a choir singer, just when he was looking for the right page to sing from, the pieces of scrap paper he used as bookmarks in his hymn book kept moving around or falling out of the book.

He was desperate to find a solution to this annoying problem.

Luckily, he worked as a researcher at 3M Corporation.

He knew about an unusual adhesive one of his colleagues had invented. It was strong enough to stick to a surface and yet easily removable. The best part was when removed, it didn't leave any residue on the surface.

He wondered what if he placed the adhesive on only one side of the scrap paper that sticks to the page, and the other side just pops out of the hymn book like a bookmark.

The idea worked.

The annoying problem had been solved.

Today, he is not the only one using his invention.

Millions of people in over 100 countries swear by it.

It's no longer a scrap paper. It's the ubiquitous "Post-It Note."

The fact that Fry worked for 3M helped. At the company, he had access to cutting edge research capabilities. But that was only the half of it.

What else helped?

He was also working for a company with the right culture.

A culture of innovation.

A culture that gave people time and freedom to explore and innovate.

In fact, the company encouraged employees to use 15 percent of their work time (yes, paid time) on "experimental doodling" — experimental projects that may turn into new products.

Fry used this "experimental doodling" time to invent the Post-It Note.

William McKnight, the legendary Chairman of 3M who inducted this 15 percent rule, once said, "If you put fences around people, you get sheep."

No one wants to be a sheep in a cubicle.

Today, everyone wants to be the GOAT — Greatest Of All Time.

So, how do you unleash innovation in your company like 3M?

By following the five-step formula: 1) be defined by the timeless versus the temporary, 2) build a culture of innovation, 3) define what innovation means to your company, 4) determine your innovation strategy, and 5) execute your innovation strategy

1. <u>Be defined by the timeless versus the temporary</u>

"Remember, you are more than your possessions," my mom advised me in 1991 as I was getting ready to migrate to the US. She is a woman of few words and rarely gives any advice, so when she does, I listen. But that wasn't always the case. Back then, I was too young and immature to understand what she meant. So I shrugged it off.

Over the years, as I went through the inevitable ups and downs of life, I often revisited what she said. When it finally sunk in, I realized the wisdom distilled in her sparse words.

If you define yourself so closely by your possessions and life's many labels (job, title, business, house, car), when you lose any of them, you also lose a piece of yourself.

But if you define yourself by your potential (experience, skills, strengths, creativity, ingenuity, perseverance), even when you lose your possessions, it's not the end of the world.

You still got the potential. With it, you can always reinvent and rebuild yourself.

You can always get another job, another title, another business, another house, another car.

Possessions are temporary. Possessions are perishable.

Potential, on the other hand, is timeless. As long as you cultivate it and put it to work, it doesn't expire. It grows. It expands.

So, what does this motherly advice have to do with the business world?

A lot.

If a business defines itself by the temporary (products, services, even business models), that's just a disaster waiting to happen.

When these products, services, and business models become obsolete (and they all do), the business itself becomes obsolete.

Remember Blockbuster?

Remember the good ole' days when if you wanted to watch a movie, you had to drive to the nearest Blockbuster to rent a movie? And then you had to remember to watch the movie in time? And then you had to remember to return the movie in time? Oh, and remember the late charges if you didn't? (There was even a rewind fee back when VHS was king!)

So, what happened to Blockbuster?

It became obsolete.

It defined itself so closely with its old economy, brick-and-mortar business model that when Netflix started offering DVD-by-mail (and eventually via streaming) and cable companies started offering movies on demand, it couldn't adapt quickly enough, it couldn't innovate fast enough. It perished.

But what if the business defines itself by the timeless? By the collective potential of its employees? By its culture of innovation?

Netflix is a great role model for this new timeless model.

In 1997, it started out as a movie by mail distribution company. In 2007, the company reinvented itself and added a streaming service. In 2013, it reinvented itself again and started producing original (not to mention award-winning) content.

In 16 years (while Blockbuster was fading away), Netflix went from mailing movies to making movies, all while amassing millions of subscribers around the world.

How did Netflix pull this off?

By being defined by the timeless and not the temporary.

This is not only limited to the media and entertainment industry. You see this play out in every single industry.

Why did Nokia and Blackberry wither away while Apple and Samsung thrived? Why did Borders Books go out of business while Amazon conquered the online market place? Why did Sears file for bankruptcy while Walmart continued its global expansion?

There is a common thread here.

Time and again, companies defined by the temporary lose out to companies defined by the timeless.

So, if your company aspires to stay relevant in this rapidly changing world, be defined by the timeless and not the temporary. Be defined by the culture of innovation and your employees' collective potential, not your existing products and services.

Or, as my mom would probably say (*in fewer words*), "Remember, you are more than your products."

2. Build a culture of innovation

How do you build a culture of innovation? Definitely not by undertaking cosmetic, random, and disjointed actions.

Companies don't become innovative by taking leaders on a week-long boondoggle to Silicon Valley, hoping the innovation they breathe in will somehow transform them and their company.

Companies don't become innovative by setting up an innovation lab, while the rest of the organization retains its hyperactive corporate immune system for any new idea.

Companies don't become innovative by acquiring an agile start-up that suffocates in its parent's rigid, slow-paced bureaucracy.

Companies don't become innovative by hosting an occasional hackathon where the winning ideas end up collecting dust at the bottom of the company's priorities.

So why do companies undertake these actions? Because they are easy. And, they help leaders create a façade of being innovative for those board meetings or employee town hall meetings.

But, do they make a company innovative? Absolutely not.

Investing in these actions and hoping it will make you an innovative company is like building a castle in the air and hoping it will survive.

Your castle needs a solid foundation to stand on.

3. Define what innovation means to your company

Remember the story about the blind men and the elephant? Each of them touched the elephant and perceived it to be a different object. The one who touched the trunk thought it was a thick snake, the one touching the ear thought it was a fan, the one touching the leg thought it was a tree trunk, and the one touching the tail thought it was a rope.

Likewise, if you search for the definition of innovation, you will find dozens of different variations. Everyone has an opinion on what it means.

Before your company can embark on a mission to become innovative, everyone on your team must agree on what your company's innovation means.

Everyone needs to agree that it's an elephant.

Everyone needs to work toward the same goal, the same outcome.

Your team will have to come up with your own definition that works for your needs, but as a starting point, you may want to use the one coined by Tim Kastelle, an author of *Handbook on the Knowledge Economy:*[2]

"Innovation is executing new ideas to create value."

That's it.

A string of key words that define innovation: "new ideas," "execution," and "create value."

You can come up with a great new idea, but if you don't execute it, you are not creating any value. That's not innovation. That's just day-dreaming.

You can come up with a great new idea and execute it. But if it doesn't create any value for your key stakeholders, that's not innovation either. That's just someone's pet project.

As Stephen Covey says, "Begin with an end in mind."

When defining your company's innovation, begin by clearly outlining what value you want to create for the stakeholders. What problem are you solving for them? What unmet need are you addressing for them?

Once you have identified the what, then you map out the how. How would you create that value? How would you solve that problem? How would you address that unmet need?

For example, Google and Uber both outlined the "what" first and then worked on the "how."

Google outlined the problem first — to organize the world's information and make it universally accessible and useful.

Then it focused on the solution — by launching initiatives such as Google Books, Google Earth, Google Maps (in addition to continuously improving its search engine).

Uber outlined an unmet customer need first — making ride-sharing easier and more convenient.

Then it focused on the how — by building its technology infrastructure, its apps for customers and drivers.

As you notice in both of these examples, technology is just a means to an end. Not an end in itself.

This is important to note because companies often get derailed in their innovation efforts because they equate technology with innovation. Simply buying and installing technology doesn't make a company innovative.

In fact, you can be innovative without investing in any new technology.

For example, when you are launching a new branding campaign, a new product marketing strategy, a new employee engagement program, a new office layout, or a new sustainability initiative, you are being innovative. You are executing new ideas that create value for your stakeholders, but none of these initiatives require investment in new technology.

So, while defining what innovation means to you and your company, don't get lost in the trees (the "how" and "means to an end"). Instead, stay laser-focused on the forest (the "what" and "the end").

As my tennis coach used to say, "Keep your eyes on the ball."

The ball here is "creating value."

4. <u>Craft your innovation strategy</u>

Let's say you have agreed to a common definition of what innovation means for your company. And, you have made sure everyone understands that the end goal is value creation for your key stakeholders.

What's next?

Determining the right innovation strategy for your company.

Your business model, your industry, your aspirations will help you decide the optimal mix of the three main innovation strategies: incremental, adjacent, and transformational.

Incremental innovation strategy focuses on making small improvements in your existing products and services. For example, think about Gillette razor. It started as a simple, single-blade razor. But over the years, in small increments, the company has added many new features and multiple blades to the razor, all while making it safer.

Adjacent innovation efforts focus on introducing new products to existing customers as well as offering existing products to new customers, new markets, and digital channels. For example, Amazon started out as an online book store but then leveraged its experience in online sales and state-of-the-art supply chain to sell practically everything to everybody.

Transformational innovation efforts focus on developing breakthroughs and inventing things for markets that don't exist yet. For example, when Apple introduced an iPhone, the market for smartphones didn't exist. The company created the market. As Steve Jobs famously said, "People don't know what they want until you show it to them."

The general rule of thumb most companies follow is 70-20-10. Meaning 70 percent of the company's innovation efforts are focused on incremental, 20 percent on adjacent, and 10 percent on transformational. But this could vary significantly from company to company. For example, a start-up trying to disrupt a market is usually 100 percent focused on transformational innovation, whereas an established incumbent (in the consumer staples industry, for instance) may focus 90 percent of its efforts on incremental innovation.

5. Execute the innovation strategy

Determining the optimal innovation strategy for your company is easy. Executing it is the hard part.

To successfully go from ideation to implementation, leaders have to answer the following questions:

- Is the innovation strategy a mission-critical part of the company's overall strategy?

People responsible for innovation can craft a brilliant innovation strategy, but if it's not one of the company's top priorities, it may end up on a back-burner. It may not receive the time, money, and resources it deserves and needs.

- Is the innovation strategy sponsored and supported by the CEO and the rest of the C-Suite?

In his first letter to employees as Microsoft's CEO, Satya Nadella wrote, "Our industry does not respect tradition — it only respects innovation." With this short sentence, he let his key stakeholders know that he would champion innovation as an important part of Microsoft's strategy moving forward.

- What is the right organizational structure to execute the innovation strategy?

If your business is homogenous and the standardization is the key to your success, then perhaps centralized innovation effort is the right approach for you.

On the other hand, if your company has disparate and distinct business units, then letting these business units own and drive their innovation efforts may more make sense.

Companies can also consider a hybrid approach where business units enjoy the autonomy to drive their innovation efforts, but these efforts across all business units are coordinated centrally.

- Do you want to create an incubator/innovation center or a new-business-opportunities group?

The primary focus of incubators and innovation centers is to generate ideas and try them out through proof of concept or prototypes. Successful prototypes require a smooth hand-over from these entities to the business units. These entities are usually cost centers.

On the other hand, the new-business-opportunities group is focused on not only generating ideas and trying out proof of concepts but also launching these proven concepts in the market and scaling them. These groups are integrated within a business unit and are considered profit centers.

- Do you have the right incentive structure for people driving innovation?

People don't do what they are asked to do, people do what they are paid to do.

If people driving innovation are incentivized on overall company performance, just like the rest of the employees, there is no incentive for them to come up with any innovative ideas, let alone test and launch them. But, if all or a significant part of their incentive pay depends on key innovation metrics such as the number of innovative ideas generated, the number of prototypes tried and tested, the number of successful market launches, they are aligned with the company's innovation strategy.

Innovation Quadrant: "Not urgent but important"

Why is innovation hard?

Because innovation is about the future. And the future always competes with the present. It always competes with the company's core business priorities.

Leaders usually have their heads in the sand dealing with the crisis of the day.

They end up living in this box where everything is "urgent and important" (and at times "urgent and not important"). They are busy *reacting* — fighting fires, managing crisis, and addressing escalations.

They don't have time to see the big waves of change swelling and gaining momentum on the horizon.

After a while, they get accustomed to this madness. They feel the false sense of comfort because their existing products are selling like hot cakes, they are expanding market share and crushing financial targets. They feel the false sense of security because they believe the box they are in will always be there.

But then one day, they wake up, and the box is gone. The competition has ripped the box apart.

Suddenly, they are exposed to the world around them. A world they are not used to. A world they haven't paid attention to.

Suddenly, the waves of change wash over the beach. The beautiful sandcastle is no more.

Another victim of the disruptive forces.

According to a McKinsey study, 75 percent of the companies currently listed in the S&P 500 will disappear by 2027.[3]

The road to the future will be littered with victims of disruptions. Victims who are myopically focused only on the "urgent and important." Victims who are spending all their energies and efforts on their existing products, services, and business models.

How do you avoid this tragic fate for your company?

By paying attention to both the "urgent and important" as well as the "not urgent but important" such as future products, services and business models.

As a company, you have to recognize the importance of your existing products and services. You have to recognize the importance of what's happening inside the box. Because it's paying the bills today. But you have to remind yourself that it won't pay the bills tomorrow.

That's why you assign a great team inside the box, making sure you are running a well-oiled machine. This team is fighting fires, managing crisis, and addressing escalations. It's also adding incremental innovations to your existing products and services.

But, you also need to have a team of leaders whose primary role is to get out on the top of the box, scanning the horizon for the ("not urgent but important") opportunities and risks.

When you get on the top of the box and look out, you realize it's a scary, brutally competitive world out there. But, you feel confident and invincible. It is not because of the safety net of the box you are sitting on, but because you have built a strong team and a strong innovation culture. A culture where people are passionate about learning, growing, adapting, and innovating.

You feel safe, not because you believe the box you are sitting on will always be there, but because you are confident that even if you lose that box in the future, your team is ready to manifest another box. A bigger, better, and smarter box.

You know the road ahead is perilous.

But, you are fully aware of what's coming your way — be it a tide, a crashing wave, or simply the unknown.

And you are prepared for it.

You are no longer a creature of disruptions but a creator of disruptions.

You are no longer the battered sandcastle.

You are the storm that crashes upon the old, to shape a new beach.

CHAPTER 12

THE FUTURE IS NEW: INSPIRE LEARNING

> *"The illiterate of the 21st century will not be those who cannot read or write, but those who cannot learn, unlearn, and relearn."*
> Alvin Toffler, Author, Futureshock

"What do I want to be today? A racecar driver? A cyborg? A warrior princess?" A young Chelsea James often mused, as she grabbed a controller and prepared to step into a new world.[1]

Video games became her portal to unleashing her imagination and creativity. She dreamed of one day creating her own video game.

Years later, thanks to a degree in marketing, she found a digital marketing job at Amazon (not exactly her dream job).

She realized that to be a game developer, she needed to have a background in software engineering. Luckily for her, Amazon had just launched a program to transition employees without a software engineering background into the company's technical roles. She applied and was chosen as one of thirty Amazonians worldwide to be a part of this pilot.

Two years of studies later, James was hired as a software engineer for Twitch, one of the world's most popular video gaming platforms.

She was ready to embrace the future. The company was ready to invest in her future.

James got to achieve her childhood dream. Amazon got one more scarcely available software engineer.

Win-win.

Nathaniel Meyers was working for AT&T in network operations in a job that was slowly disappearing. Luckily for him, his employer had partnered with Georgia Tech to prepare its employees for the future.[2]

For qualified employees, the company paid for an online master's degree in computer science from the university. Meyers qualified for the opportunity and completed his degree in two years. Working full-time, tending to his family duties, and finishing a graduate degree was a herculean undertaking. But in the end, it was all worth it as he landed a much-coveted data scientist job within the company.

He was ready to embrace the future. The company was ready to invest in his future.

Meyers got to upgrade his education. AT&T got one more scarcely available data scientist.

Win-win.

James and Meyers are not alone.

In 2019, Amazon pledged $700 million to upskill 100,000 of its US-based employees by 2025 and prepare them for the in-demand jobs for the future.[3] In addition to helping non-technical employees to transition into software engineering, this initiative also trains fulfillment center employees (roles quickly disappearing due to automation) to move into technical roles. Even employees who already have technical backgrounds can upskill themselves for an AI-driven world by developing machine learning skills.

A few years ago, AT&T realized that only half of its 250,000 employees had the necessary science, technology, engineering, and math skills the company required. More importantly, 40 percent of its workers were busy with jobs related to hardware issues, which were likely to disappear over the next decade.

So, in 2018, AT&T pledged $1 billion for a multi-year initiative called "Future Ready" to prepare its workforce for tomorrow.[4] The initiative includes a career center that allows its employees to identify and train for the kinds of jobs the company needs today and down the road. The company also offers free courses to qualified employees in collaboration with Coursera, Udacity, and leading universities such as Georgia Tech and the University of Notre Dame.

Why are companies investing so much time, effort, and money in upskilling and reskilling efforts?

Workforce disruption is underway

According to a recent McKinsey study, by 2030, up to 375 million jobs globally could be completely eliminated due to automation.[5] However, numerous studies, including the one by McKinsey, predict that over the next decade, the number of new jobs created will be higher than the number of jobs lost due to automation.

We have seen this movie before.

This time is no different. Except, this time around, we don't have decades to upskill and reskill.

The speed of displacement is significantly faster. If we want to keep the global economic engine humming, we need to avoid mass unemployment. We need to proactively prepare for and respond to this workforce disruption by having effective and timely reskilling programs in place.

And the onus is not just on the Amazons or the AT&Ts of the world. They are not the only ones impacted or feeling the pain.

Everyone is.

AI doesn't care how big or small your company is. If it can do things better, faster, cheaper, and smarter, it will show up at your doorstep. If you turn a blind eye to it, if you live in denial and pretend it doesn't exist, it's just a matter of time before you don't exist.

It's like a giant wave that keeps swelling by the day. Those who pay attention to it and prepare for it will ride it and thrive. The ones who turn their back to it and ignore it will drown.

How do you ride this wave of change? How do you thrive?

Invest in your most important asset: your employees

Your employees are eager to embrace the future.

They are ready to walk through the *right* door that leads to the *right* future.

A few self-actualized employees may find this door on their own and unlock it. But the rest may need your guidance as to what door to open (direction) and your help in unlocking the door (training) itself.

The question is, do you — as leaders — know what door to open? And how to unlock it?

You don't want the blind leading the blind.

As a company, do you know...

How technology and automation will transform today's jobs into tomorrow's?

Which jobs will be in more demand?

Which jobs will become obsolete?

What part of each job may be automated?

What will your employees do with the time freed up through automation?

Which jobs will be augmented by AI?

How will you train your employees to partner with AI?

Are you able to envision the new job types you may need in the future that don't exist yet?

What part of your future workforce will be made up of your current workforce that has been reskilled and retrained?

What part of your future workforce will be made up of new hires?

What part of your future workforce will be made up of freelancers?

What part of your future workforce will come from mergers and acquisitions?

Clearly, the future may not be clear to you to answer many of these questions. But, it's good to go through the exercise and at least have a sense as to where you are heading. It's good to have an appreciation for how you will need to change and adapt as the future unfolds.

Once you have answered these questions, once you have selected the right door and know how to unlock it, your employees will be there to line up behind you.

It's up to you whether they stay where they are, remain illiterate, and become obsolete *(with you)*, or they walk through the door to relearn and conquer the future *(for you)*.

New age, New approach

New challenges call for new solutions.

It's time to revamp, redesign, and renew your Learning and Development (LD) efforts.

Traditionally, a company's LD efforts are tactical and reactive — focused on skills needed by the company *today*. Going forward, companies also need to be strategic and proactive — also focusing on skills needed in 5 to 10 years down the road.

Traditionally, a company's LD efforts are static – year after year, offering and delivering the same learning modules. Going forward, these efforts will need to be dynamic – constantly evolving and changing to keep up with (and ideally stay ahead of) the needs of the business.

Traditionally, a company's LD delivery has been single-dimensional — mainly through instructors in person. Going forward, it needs to be multidimensional — leveraging instructors, online modules, peer-to-peer training, external speakers, on-demand training from companies such as Coursera or Udacity, among others.

Traditionally, a company's LD efforts are an afterthought driven by a small department far removed from the C-suite. Going forward, these efforts will need to be a foreword prepared and practiced by the CEO and the senior leaders.

Do you want your employees to embrace continuous learning? Show them how you are acquiring new skills, how you are sharpening your saw, how you are working on the "future you." If they see you learning, they will follow suit.

Five learning priorities for the decade ahead

1. <u>Bridge the gap between today's skills and tomorrow's requirements</u>

First and foremost, companies will need to create a holistic ecosystem that promotes, facilitates, and manifests learning for all four types of resources affected by AI and automation:

One...the employees whose jobs are safe but would like to proactively upskill or reskill for the "in-demand" jobs of tomorrow. Think about Chelsea James. Her job in digital marketing was futureproof, but the company allowed her to reskill for an "in-demand" job for the future — software engineer.

Two...the employees whose jobs are at risk of displacement. Think about Nathaniel Meyers. His job in network operations was fading away, but the company gave him an opportunity to reskill himself to become a data scientist and stay relevant.

Three...the employees whose jobs will not be displaced but altered by AI. The McKinsey study concluded that for every 6 out of 10 jobs, 30 percent of the work could be automated using currently available technology. If AI frees up a significant part of your employees' time doing the mundane and repetitive tasks, how would you reskill them to create more value?

Four...the freelancers who are working on long-term projects for your company. They are not your full-time employees, but they are mission-critical for your future success. While you are not required to provide any training to them, it may be in your interest to keep them up to date with their skills. This investment may entice them for a longer partnership or even full-time employment.

2. Unleash the human in your employees

It's time for the companies to let humans reclaim what it means to be human.

Yes, you read it right.

Think about the paradox we have created.

We are spending billions of dollars trying to make artificial intelligence more human.

We are giving chatbots names and personalities.

We are making Alexa and Siri more empathetic.

We are refining the facial expressions of "Sophia" — the humanoid robot, so she can emote.

We are teaching machines how to paint a masterpiece or compose like Mozart.

And yet, what do we do with employees after we hire them?

We spend billions turning these real people into automatons. We give them a number. We ask them to badge in their personality and fit in. We put fences — both virtual and physical — around them as to what they can or cannot do. We program them with rules and regulations, policies and procedures. We sap their creativity. We suffocate the song within them.

How can we stop this madness?

No, we can't stop the efforts to humanize AI. That train has left the station.

But, what we can do is to reclaim and unleash the human in each one of us.

One day, AI may match human prowess in all its glory. But, for the next decade, we will continue to have a significant edge against the machines when it comes to our inherent human skills and talents.

Companies often spend most of their LD efforts developing technical skills such as coding, programming, or data analysis. Going forward, developing soft skills — such as being empathetic, being creative, being innovative, and being inspiring — will become equally important, if not more.

3. <u>Learn to leverage the complementary strengths of AI</u>

We have a choice. Either we consider AI as a foe or as a friend. Either we think it diminishes our role or augments it. Either we create a culture where everyone is afraid of it, or everyone is excited to partner with it.

To thrive in the decade ahead, we have to recognize how AI complements us. We have to create a culture where everyone is aware of the complementary strengths AI brings to the table. We have to teach our employees how to leverage AI so that it rounds out human efforts.

For example...

Leverage AI for efficiency. *For doing things right.* AI can help us manufacture products better, faster, cheaper, and smarter.

Leverage people for effectiveness. *For doing the right things.* People can decide *what to* manufacture, utilizing our creativity, originality, ingenuity, and intuition.

Leverage AI for IQ. To analyze, to synthesize.

Leverage people for EQ. To inspire, to empathize.

Leverage AI for small. For precision and accuracy.

Leverage people for big. For strategy and vision.

Leverage AI for stamina. 24 hours a day. 7 days a week. 365 days a year.

Leverage people for wisdom. Knowing when to pause.

4. <u>Instill out of the box thinking</u>

Google is known for its generous perks for its employees. Free chef-prepared meals, micro-kitchens filled with snacks, free shuttles, foosball tables, just to name a few.

However, the one perk I find most appealing is having an opportunity to meet with and listen to the world's most influential thinkers, creators, and leaders in the series called "Talks at Google."

What's fascinating about this series is that most guest speakers have nothing to do with Google's business model. Most of them probably can't even define what deep learning is.

Luminaries like Lady Gaga, David Beckham, Hillary Clinton, and Paul Krugman have all been featured in this series.

The topics cover everything under the sun and beyond. They range from unexciting (tax strategies for the savvy real estate investor) to exciting (how to make a spaceship), from esoteric (forbidden archeology) to intriguing (your playlist can change your life), from foodie (the Pizza Bible) to funny (100 tricks to appear smart in meetings).[6]

What does Google get out of this?

A lot.

We spend a lot of our time in a box. Where day after day, we end up working with the same people (who are just like us with identical education and experience). Where we end up working on the same projects and products. Where we end up encountering the same challenges and complications. Where we end up coming up with the same suggestions and solutions.

Soon, this box becomes an incestuous breeding ground, sprouting only myopia and staleness (exactly the opposite of what you need to be innovative).

Often, the inspiration for your next product, next marketing campaign, next feature comes when you get out of the box.

In the fall of 2007, we had invited Janet Belarmino to speak with over 1,000 of our Philippines-based leaders. She had a fascinating and inspiring story to share with us. She was one of the first Filipino women to climb Mount Everest.

Her story was also timely because, at that time, we were climbing our own Mount Everest. We had set a goal of growing our company four-fold within three years (specifically, that meant we had to go from 6,000 employees to over 24,000 employees).

When Janet spoke to us, we were just getting started on our journey. Every time we looked up at the summit and thought of getting to the goal of 24,000 employees, we felt overwhelmed. We thought we would never get there. We wanted to give up.

But Janet had a solution for our anxiety.

She said when climbing Mount Everest, she hardly ever looked up at the summit. Because every time she looked up, it looked so distant, so high, so steep, so overwhelming. It looked beyond her reach.

Instead, she focused all her effort and energy on what was within her reach — the next step. She took that next step and then the next and the next.

She didn't know anything about running a Business Process Outsourcing company. But she knew how to set an audacious goal and achieve it (take one step, then another).

Not every company has Google's gravitas to attract the Lady Gagas or David Beckhams of this world.

But there are Janet Belarminos in every community, city, and country.

These are ordinary people manifesting as extra-ordinary.

Seek them out.

Often, the "AHA" moment comes when you are listening to others sharing their stories and struggles, their trials and triumphs, their passion, and their purpose.

5. Desire and drive > Degrees and diplomas

What do Richard Branson, Henry Ford, Walt Disney, and my dad have in common? They are all high school dropouts.

Unlike others on the list above, my dad is not a hero to millions. But he is a hero to me. He grew up in a small remote village in India. When he was 14, my grandfather passed away, and he had to drop out of school to help support his family.

He didn't have any degree or diploma. But he had the desire and drive to learn. He self-taught himself how to communicate in English (the first one in his family) and how to lead people (the first one in his family). By the time he retired, he was an award-winning executive looking after hundreds of people.

There are people like my dad everywhere in the workplace, and the numbers are growing.

In the past, people often skipped formal education because they didn't have a choice. Either they couldn't afford it, or they had to attend to other obligations.

Now, many of the Gen Zers are skipping higher education *despite having a choice.*

A survey found that 75 percent of Gen Zers say there are other ways of getting a good education than going to college.[7] Many of them are looking for employers who will provide them with state-of-the-art training that is relevant in this fast-changing world.

They have the desire and drive.

They just don't have the patience (or money) to spend precious years of their lives in a slow-moving antiquated education system.

So, what does this mean for you?

If your LD efforts only focus on the elites — the ones with formal education, if it only invests in them, if it only upskills them, if it only opens doors for them, you are leaving so much raw energy and talent on the table.

Companies that recognize and harness this pure potential will create significantly more value than the companies that don't.

Be on the lookout for people who may not have the pedigree, but they have the passion.

They may not have the resume, but they have the resolve.

With proper mentoring and training, they can become the next set of engineers, innovators, marketers, and leaders you so desperately need.

This year, my dad will turn 83. He has adapted to the digital age better than most people I know. He has built a nice business on eBay buying and selling rare and precious coins of the world. He has achieved a respectable "Purple Star" rating on the platform.

When I asked him why he was working so hard, he said he is gunning for the "Silver Shooting Star" — the best rating given on eBay.

Drive and desire are greater than degrees or diplomas. I know it first-hand.

CHAPTER 13

THE FUTURE IS FUN: ENJOY EXPEDITION

> *"The business of business is people."*
> Herb Kelleher, Co-founder,
> Southwest Airlines

"Can I pretend to have your attention for just a few moments?" the voice blared over the PA system as the aircraft was departing the gate.[1]

Passengers assumed this would be just another boring safety announcement that they had heard a million times before, so they ignored it.

But Martha Cobb—the flight attendant making the announcement— had other plans for her seemingly mundane task.

She pointed to her colleagues in the aisle and continued, "My ex-husband, my new boyfriend, and their divorce attorney are going to show you the safety features of the Boeing 737 800 series."

This got their attention. As a handful of people broke into laughter, the majority looked forward, and even the laggards removed their headphones to see what had their fellow passengers smiling and paying attention.

As for Martha, she was just getting started.

For the next 3 minutes, she sprinkled the safety spiel with her own unique dash of humor.

"It's a no smoking, no whining, no complaining flight."

"If you are traveling with small children, we are sorry. If you are traveling with more than one child, pick out the one you think might have the most earning potential down the road."

"If there is anything we can do to make your flight more enjoyable, please tell us — just as soon as we land in Salt Lake City. And if there is anything you can do to make our flight more enjoyable, we will tell you immediately."

When Cobb was done, the entire cabin broke into sustained cheers and applause. The video of her announcement was posted on YouTube and has been watched over 25 million times.

If you witnessed this on any other airline, you would be worried about her job.

But this was Southwest Airlines.

The company where the co-founder Herb Kelleher himself once came to a company gathering dressed like Elvis Presley.[2]

The company where people are hired for their personality *and encouraged to bring it to work.*

At Southwest, Cobb is not an exception. She is the norm.

A lack of uniformity is not a bug, it's a feature.

All of her 60,000+ colleagues come to work fully empowered to have fun with their customers and co-workers. And they all do. In their own individual ways.

It's not surprising to see a flight attendant climbing into an overhead compartment to greet passengers as they board.

It's not surprising to see an entire cabin clapping while the flight attendant raps the announcements.

It's not surprising to see a gate agent playing games with passengers (like whose driver's license photo is the worst) to kill time when a flight gets delayed.

Does Southwest give out a manual for this? No. (How could they?)

This is just employees being themselves. This is just employees having a great time with each other and with their customers.

Sounds like all play and no work?

Not at all.

Collectively, these empowered employees have built one of the most profitable, most awarded, and most admired airline companies in the world.

In an industry notorious for financial troubles (over 100 bankruptcies in the US alone since 1978), Southwest outshines the competition with 47 consecutive years of profitability.[3]

In an industry often derided as a synonym for poor customer service, Southwest has become one of the most awarded airlines for customer satisfaction. In 2020, this non-traditional company was voted as the best airline by JD Power in its annual North American Airline Satisfaction Study.[4]

In an industry known for its high employee burnout, Southwest loses only four percent of its employees annually.[5]

It's been featured on Fortune's annual list of most admired companies since 2009.[6] And for every two job openings, it attracts 100 applicants.

So how did Kelleher create this all-around remarkable success story? Did he have extensive experience in the aviation industry?

No.

He didn't know anything about running an airline.

But he knew a thing or two about leading people.

He knew that each one of us is unique.

He knew that if he took care of his people, they would take care of his business.

So, he led Southwest as if the business of his business was its people.

In turn, people proved him right.

They made it their business to take care of their business (as if it was their own business).

He built the stage. The people performed magic.

Year after year.

For 47 years and counting.

Why is work a recurring nightmare for so many?

In Chapters 3 and 4, we covered how the digital generations aspire to pursue entrepreneurial ventures and how people of all ages are attracted to the freelance lifestyle.

But what's driving these growing trends?

Perhaps it's our innate yearning to have freedom.

Freedom to decide what we want to do, how we want to do it, where we want to do it, when we want to do it, and with whom we want to do it.

But for many of us, this freedom is elusive.

That's why our work week starts with the depressing "Monday morning blues" and ends with the joyous "TGIF!"

When asked, "Do you experience elevated anxiety on Sunday in anticipation of Monday?" an astonishing 81 percent of the workers answered, "yes," according to research by The Sleep Judge.[7] In fact, we don't crack our first smile until 11:16 am on Monday morning[8] (and that's probably because the lunch break is only 44 minutes away).

In another study, people associated Monday with words "boring" and "tired" and Friday with words "freedom" and "release."

"Freedom" and "Release?" Aren't these the words used to describe the final days of a prison term?

Subliminally (or maybe even vocally), that's what we think of work. A recurring weekly prison sentence that begins on Monday and ends with Friday.

No wonder people dread going to work.

When full-time was the only option

Like the generations before them, Baby Boomers and Gen Xers didn't like this 9-to-5 drudgery either.

But they didn't have a choice.

They could have started their own business, sure, but starting a bricks and mortar business in the old economy was hard, to say the least. And sustaining it was even harder.

Finding a job was the easiest way to make a living. That's what the Jones' did. So, their neighbors did too. They got used to this dichotomous, schizophrenic, and head-spinning life—depressing work weeks followed by short joyful weekends.

But the world is changing.

The old economy is giving way to the new. Old guards are on their way out, and the entrepreneurs are rolling in.

And these new generations are made from a different cloth. They don't fathom the concept of hard starts on Mondays and the hard stops on Fridays. For them, life is more fluid. Work and pleasure co-exist and co-mingle all the time.

During 9 to 5, these fluidity experts may want to take a break to walk their dogs, volunteer for a cause, run some errands, or simply catch up on social media.

But don't panic. When you call it a day at 5 pm and go home to watch Monday Night Football or to binge on your favorite Netflix show, they will work through the evening if they need to. They will get the job done. But on their terms.

Yes, they are different. And different is notoriously difficult.

Do you have to put up with different?

Yes, you do.

Remember, by the end of this new decade, these digital generations will make up about 67 percent of the global workforce, while the Baby Boomers will be phased out of the workforce.

Full-time is no longer the only option

In the past, companies could get away with rigid rules, lackluster leaders, prehistoric policies, and boring bureaucracies.

Question: "Where would employees go anyway?"

Answer: "To the company next door? It's the same banana over there!"

Now, it's different.

As an employer, you are no longer the only game in town. You have (at least) two new competitors.

One…you are competing not just with other companies, but also with your employees' entrepreneurial aspirations. With just a smartphone, laptop, and an Internet connection, they can launch their own entrepreneurial venture or be a freelancer.

Two…you are competing with companies not just in your city, but with the companies around the world. Being a full-time remote employee has never been easier. Why would employees settle for less when they can find their perfect match globally (while staying home in their pajamas)?

You can no longer be complacent with "It's the same banana everywhere else." Because that idea is dead.

People can now find frozen bananas, chocolate-dipped bananas, ice-cream bananas with sprinkles, and fried banana rolls dipped in honey. Why would anyone settle for just a plain banana?

Time for a massive reset

It is time for you to rethink, reimagine, and redesign the kind of company you want to be.

And the kind of company where others would want to be.

The company that offers what the employees are looking for. Not just a mere job, but an expedition.

An expedition where employees will have the autonomy to chart their course. Where they will have the freedom to explore and create. Where they will have the flexibility to do it on their terms.

Offering autonomy, freedom, and flexibility is easy.

Finding the sweet spot between autonomy and accountability, between freedom and fences, and between flexibility and framework is hard.

Companies like Spotify, Netflix, Google, and Amazon are exemplary role models for how to strive for this sweet spot. And, in turn, achieve spectacular success.

How do they do that?

By creating an environment where "intrapreneurs" can flourish and express themselves. Where these enterprising employees can have the best of both worlds. An opportunity and freedom to be creative and to put their entrepreneurial spirit to work while having the safety and security of a full-time job.

Essentially, creating an environment where they can have their cake and eat it too.

It's a win for companies also.

They get to hire and retain the best of what these generations have to offer. You have to match the young and feisty on the outside with young and feisty on the inside.

To create the culture of intrapreneurship, to create an environment where people can enjoy the expedition, you have to do three things: renovate your organizational structure, empower autonomy to your employees, and enhance trust within your company.

1. <u>Renovating organization structure</u>

GM surpassed Ford in 1929 and remained the top automaker in the world for the following 70 years. Kodak dominated its industry for all of the 20th century. Macy's, Bloomingdale, and Sears ruled the retail world for over a century.

(Notice how all of these achievements are past tense?)

In the last century, companies have remained relevant for decades. Companies dominated markets for decades.

It was a different world.

Back then, the pace of change was slow, and the pace of disruption even slower.

Back then, stability mattered more than speed. ("Let's not rock the boat!")

Back then, slow and deliberate trumped fast and furious. ("Slow and easy wins the race!")

Back then, maintaining the status quo was rewarded more than trying new things. ("No one got fired for saying no!")

Back then, getting it right the first time was rewarded more than learning lessons from failing. ("Who wants to deliver the bad news to the boss?")

Back then, empires and silos won over collaboration and teamwork. ("Turf wars!")

These behaviors sprouted from and were nurtured by the top-down, hierarchical, rigid, and siloed organization structure.

But this structure has run its course.

Now, the pace of change and disruption is accelerating.

Now, if we don't rock the boat ourselves, others will (and perhaps capsize it).

Now, slow and easy gets eaten by the fast and furious (and they are hungrier than ever).

Now, if we keep saying no to new ideas, forget about getting fired, there will be no company left to be fired from.

Now, if we are not bold enough to try, fail, and learn, if we are not bold enough to deliver the bad news to the boss, the market will.

Now, no more "Turf wars" within the company. There is only one war. The one with the competition.

It's time to create an organization structure that accelerates innovation, experimentation, and learning. It's time to tear down the walls and remove the silos. It's time to demolish unnecessary layers and flatten the organization. It's time to decentralize decision making. It's time to engage employees with autonomy.

Now is the time.

2. <u>Empowering autonomy</u>

How did Spotify go from zero to 130 million paying subscribers in 12 years?

By turning the entire company into one big innovation lab with hundreds of cross-functional, autonomous, self-organizing teams working as *mini startups*.[9]

Each of these mini startups — called squads — is made up of around 8 people from a variety of disciplines and has the autonomy to determine what to build, how to build, and even how to organize while building it.

Essentially, the company empowers these squads to take full ownership of the lean start-up process of "Think it. Build it. Ship it. Tweak it." The main goal is to enhance customer experience by frequently releasing new features for their platform.

Most companies keep all their employees neatly organized in silos and layers on one big giant ship, making it horribly slow and extremely hard to maneuver.

Spotify, on the other hand, deploys these mini startups in smaller, faster, and agile speedboats. Each speedboat is autonomous but aligned with the overarching mission of the mothership. Each speedboat ready to change its course, its direction, its speed, its mission on a dime, like a flock of starlings wheeling in the sky.

Just take a moment and compare the speed and velocity of Spotify's structure with yours?

Spotify is not the only one who has deployed these speedboats. Companies like Google, Amazon, and Netflix have all adopted this agile way of organizing, innovating, and working.

And needless to say, it has turned them into talent magnets. Spotify receives over 350,000 resumes a year.[10] Google receives 50,000 resumes a week.[11]

Everyone wants to get off the slow and suffocating mothership and get on a fast and liberating speedboat.

Who wouldn't want to have autonomy and ownership?

Who wouldn't want to chart their own course?

Who wouldn't want to ride the waves and create their own expedition?

These examples of young digital players may beg the question: can traditional companies still be agile? Can traditional companies shake off the lethargy and complacency that comes with their deep-rooted history and slow-paced bureaucracy?

Well, yes, but the better question to ask is: will these traditional companies survive without being agile?

Highly unlikely.

In this digital age, the battle for the market share has become asymmetric. It's no longer just Goliath taking a bite or two from another Goliath. Now it's the David stealing the entire lunch (forever) from Goliath.

In the past, a company's illustrious history, formidable size, and reassuring stability used to be its strengths. Now they are liabilities.

Goliaths are starting to realize that they need to stop scratching their heads and match David's agility.

That's what ING did.

ING is one of the top 30 banks globally with an illustrious history that traces back to the 19th century.

A few years ago, ING leaders realized that it could no longer survive just being a Goliath (a mere financial services company). It had to cultivate David's nimbleness by being a technology company operating in the financial services industry.[12]

Just like Amazon is a technology company operating in retail industry.

Just like Spotify and Netflix are technology companies operating in the media and entertainment industry.

So, what did ING leaders do? They studied and visited the companies they admired — the likes of Spotify, Google, and Netflix — and borrowed a chapter from their book.

In 2015, ING embraced an agile organizational structure. It completely reorganized the mothership in the Netherlands and deployed a majority of its employees in hundreds of speed boats in cross-functional, self-organizing, autonomous but aligned mini startups.

The gambit paid off.

Employees felt empowered, and they embraced the autonomy that came with the new agile structure. Within months, employee engagement improved significantly.

Customers appreciated the proactive and responsive new organization. With more frequent software releases and updates, customer satisfaction scores moved up multiple points.

Most importantly, this new organizational structure cultivated a company culture that started to match David's agility and nimbleness.

Who said Goliaths couldn't dance?

3. <u>Enhancing trust</u>

Paul Zak, the author of the book *Trust Factor*, has been fascinated by how trust impacts company performance for over two decades.

After several years of study, he derived a mathematical relationship between trust and economic performance in 2001. Then he spent years researching if there is a direct correlation between trust and oxytocin — the hormone that, among other things, promotes empathy and general well-being in people. His research confirmed that higher trust among people produced higher oxytocin in them.[13]

A bit nerdy? Yes.

But insightful? Absolutely.

His study concluded that compared with people at low-trust companies, people at high-trust companies report 74 percent less stress, 106 percent more energy at work, and 76 percent more engagement.

Even if we didn't come across Zak's work or his book, we *intuitively* know that when we are working with people we trust, we are happier.

And the opposite is also true.

Working in a company where bosses micromanage their employees won't make us happy.

Working in a company where "information is power" and bosses hoard it from the rest won't make us happy.

Working in a company where "we are to be seen but not heard" won't make us happy.

But at companies like Netflix, Buffer, and Amazon, bosses have cracked the code on creating a culture of trust where people are happier.

Netflix hires the top talent it can find and then trusts these people to do what is best for Netflix.[14]

Its travel and entertainment policy is only five words long: "act in Netflix's best interest."

Its vacation policy is only two words long: "take vacation."

The company believes that when people are trusted to make the right decision, they cultivate a sense of responsibility and self-discipline. They act as if it were their own company.

Buffer, a 10-year-old start-up with 85 employees offering social media tools, has built a culture of trust by embracing unparalleled transparency.[15]

Buffer's number one value is "Default to transparency," and it has put practically anything you want to know about the company in the public domain.

Want to know how much these employees (including the CEO) make? All salary data is available on a Google spreadsheet in the public domain.

Want information on diversity and inclusion data for its employees? It's available online for anyone to see.

Want to use the code developed by the company? It's available for free for anyone to use.

Buffer believes "information is power." *But only when it's shared with others.*

Amazon builds trust by creating an environment where people's ideas and viewpoints are not only respected but acted upon. The company has built a culture where employees have "multiple paths to yes" for getting approvals for their ideas.[16] Even if your boss says no to your idea, you can pitch it to your boss's boss or other senior executives in the company. There are incidences when Jeff Bezos himself said "no" to an idea, but it was acted upon because other executives in the company thought it was worth a try.

At Amazon, your voice matters. Your ideas matter. You are expected to be seen *and* heard.

At Amazon, there are many gatekeepers, and the key is to let the best idea in and win.

Maybe, as a company, it's too much for you to adapt a two-word vacation policy or to put everyone's salaries in the public domain or to give people the freedom to go around their supervisors.

But you don't have to get there overnight.

You just have to start the journey toward more trust. And along the way, find a spot that works for you.

In this digital age, running a company is like flying a jumbo jet through one storm after another. You don't control the turbulence that you encounter. You don't control what the competition will do next. You don't control when the next pandemic will strike. You don't control when the recession will resurface.

But you do control whether you and your team will relish this bumpy ride or not.

You do control whether your cabin is empowered or demoralized.

You do control whether this becomes a journey of a lifetime or a recurring Monday to Friday nightmare of the mundane.

Flying through the storms is tough. Leading a company through treacherous terrain is tough. Why make it any tougher?

Enjoy the expedition.

Or, as Martha Cobb would say, "Now, sit back and relax or sit up and be tense, either way, it will take the same amount of time to get to Salt Lake City."

I bet her oxytocin level is high.

THE FUTURE: GROWTH OR EXTINCTION

> "At any given moment, we have two choices: to step forward into growth or to step back into safety."
> Abraham Maslow

"Athletics is not so much about the legs," Eliud Kipchoge quipped. "It's about the heart and mind."

Kipchoge would know. After all, he has won 12 of the 13 marathons he has entered and is the current world record holder with a time of 2:01:39 set at the 2018 Berlin Marathon.[1]

What's his secret to success?

Does he have a silver bullet?

No, he doesn't have "a" silver bullet.

He plans and prepares for each marathon *holistically – physically, nutritionally, and mentally*.[2]

Before every race, he undergoes intense physical preparation, including gym workouts, aerobics, strength, and conditioning.

For the main part of his training, he moves into a special training camp in Kaptagat, Kenya – a region 8,000 feet above the sea-level. Like other elite athletes, he likes to practice at a higher altitude and compete at a lower altitude.

The terrain around the training camp is unforgiving, and the air is thin. Most people would run out of breath after a leisurely jog. But, Kipchoge logs 130 miles per week.

While he works out harder, he also tries to recover harder. He takes a nap between his morning and afternoon runs. Every week, he receives three massages, a physiotherapy session, and a couple of ice baths to soothe those tired muscles.

To keep up with this intense physical regimen, Kipchoge requires a lot of energy. Nutritionally, he sticks to a simple diet based on cornmeal porridge and vegetables. The meal provides him with minerals, fiber, and healthy carbohydrates, slowly releasing energy into his body.

While running, he complements this diet with Maurten's Hydrogels. The body dissolves the sugar in these gels within the hour, which quickly refuels his body during a race.

Kipchoge also spends a lot of time conditioning his mind.[3] He is not wishy-washy about his goals. Once he sets his sight on a goal, he singularly focuses on it. He convinces himself that he is capable of achieving this goal.

He says, "Mental fitness plays a big role during competition. If you don't rule your mind, your mind will rule you."[4] To cultivate and maintain a positive frame of mind, he ends the day reading inspirational books.

What's the output of this holistic preparation? A 5.6 feet, 115 pound, lean and mean machine. The greatest marathon runner of the modern era.[5]

What can we learn from Kipchoge about futureproofing our careers and our companies?

One very important point: The future is also a marathon — the one that never ends.

To win this race, just like Kipchoge, we must plan and prepare holistically. We must fire on all cylinders. Not just the legs, but also the heart and the mind.

If you want to futureproof your career, you must do *all* of the five things we discussed in Section II:

1. The future is AI. Be the kind of human that AI cannot replicate. Enhance your EQ. If you are creative, learn to be analytical. If you are analytical, learn to be creative. Fire up your whole brain — left and right. Be a pony with many tricks. Travel on many roads and learn to notice the magic that happens at the intersections.
2. The future is change. Embrace change and be a catalyst for it. Cultivate muscles to say "no more" to mediocrity, nonsensical, and unfair. Create value by influencing and championing positive change.
3. The future is people. Be an alchemist who inspires ordinary people to achieve extraordinary feats. Unshackle the chains of complacency and take a leap toward greatness. Recognize and reveal the gold lying within you and those around you.
4. The future is turbulent. Be a captain with the nerves of steel. Display grace under fire. Companies and industries are becoming obsolete. Jobs and skills are becoming

irrelevant. Disruptive forces are gaining strength. Navigate through this treacherous terrain with poise and clarity.
5. The future is unknown. Be a futurist and envision possible futures. Yogi Bera once said, "It's hard to predict, especially the future." Yes, it's hard but not impossible. You are surrounded by clues as to how the future may unfold. Pay attention to these clues, study them, synthesize them, and then extrapolate.

To futureproof your company, you must prepare holistically doing all of the five things we covered in Section III:

1. The future is digital. Transform the business to lead your industry. This transformation is not about technology. It's about solving problems, creating value, enhancing customer experience, and improving employee engagement. It is about tweaking or completely revamping your business model. It's about being the disruptor and not the disrupted.
2. The future is meaningful. Instill purpose that guides your company like the true North. Your customers and employees want to know what you stand for before they stand with you. Define your purpose and let it animate everything you do. Today, Corporate Social Responsibility can no longer just be a part of the strategy, but it should be the strategy.
3. The future is boundless. Unleash a culture of innovation to take advantage of these opportunities. Companies married to the temporary — products, services, and business models — will face extinction. Companies married to the timeless — skills, talents, and agility of their employees — will thrive. Define what innovation means to your company. Craft your innovation strategy and then flawlessly execute it.

4. **The future is new.** Inspire learning to prepare your workforce for tomorrow. Some of your employees may require upskilling. Others may require complete reskilling. Almost all of them will need training on how to better partner with AI. Many Gen Zers may not come with the degrees you are looking for, but they have the desire to learn. They are counting on you to provide them with the relevant training.
5. **The future is fun.** The journey ahead is hard, arduous, demanding, and stressful. But, it's up to you whether your employees enjoy the ride or not. Create a culture based on trust where employees can find a sweet spot between autonomy and accountability, between freedom and fences, and between flexibility and framework. Become a talent magnet by making it a journey of a lifetime for your employees.

Yes, futureproofing is a lot of work. It's never easy to change, grow, adapt, transform.

But, what's the alternative?

Remember what Maslow said? At any given moment, you have a choice: either step forward into growth or step back into safety.

In today's rapidly changing world, the word safety has a new synonym: *Extinction*.

So, *growth or extinction* is the choice.

Remember Alaska's pink salmon, Florida's green lizards, and New York City's bed bugs? What do they all have in common?

They all chose growth.

I hope you do too.

DOWNLOAD A FREE FRAMEWORK

As a thank you for purchasing this book,
I'd like to offer you a FREE two-page framework
that summarizes the key takeaways from the book.
You may print it and keep it close to you for easy reference.

Please download the free framework here:
https://framework.futureproofyourcareerandcompany.com/

THANK YOU

First of all, thank you for purchasing this book. I know you could have picked up any number of books to read, but you picked this book, and for that, I am genuinely grateful.

If you enjoyed this book and found some benefit reading this, I'd like to hear from you and hope that you could take some time to post a review on my Amazon Book Page.

As a first-time author, I would greatly appreciate your feedback and support.

I would also like to invite you to stay in touch with me.

Please visit my website www.maulikparekh.com and join me on my social media channels.

Wishing you a flourishing future,

Maulik

ACKNOWLEDGMENTS

To my wife, Tonichi…without your unwavering support and encouragement, this book would not be possible. As a first-time author, I was on shaky ground, but you were my rock. As the Chief *Everything* Officer for this passion project, you helped manifest this dream into reality. Thank you also for being my "audible" and reading my lame initial drafts with so much passion and making them sound like they were award-winning prose!

To Pernita Clara…the idea for the book was conceived as you arrived in our lives four years ago. Because of you, the future became more meaningful. Your natural curiosity and a sense of wonder inspired me to change the way I look at the world. Thank you for always looking for an opportunity to type gibberish in the manuscript when I wasn't looking!

To Arusha Savannah…most of the book was written after you were born a year ago. When I needed a break, I looked for you. Gazing into your big beautiful eyes and an infectious smile nourished my soul. Thank you for waking me up at 4:30 am every morning with your loud, shrill, and incessant screams. I didn't need an alarm (neither did our neighbors) for my morning writing ritual.

To my parents (to whom this book is dedicated to), Deepti, Jyoti, Raj, Omika, Rishika, Aashika...I am grateful for your support, your best wishes, and blessings over the years. You gave me the freedom to fail and fly. You gave me the space to stumble and soar. Space is the most sublime but the most difficult manifestation of love. Without it, this book would not be possible.

To Jun, Jinky, Evelyn, Cliff, Linda, Ed, Paolo, Dani, Issa, Archie, Igge, Jen, Chai, Hannah...thank you for adopting me as one of your own and warmly welcoming me in your life. Your kindness has deeply touched my heart. Because of you, no matter where I am in the world, the Philippines will always remain as my home sweet home!

To Manny Pangilinan...you are my mentor, champion, and a source of inspiration. Thank you for your encouragement for this undertaking and sharing your wisdom along the way.

To Ken Tuchman, Chris McCann, Linda Green-Kiely, Brian Delaney, Chad Carlson, Takashi Amino, Shinya Imai, Toru Izuta, Sigit Prasetya, Brian Hong, Puneet Shivam, Sanjiv Vohra, Francis Kong, Roger Kidwell, Kylie Luo, Benedict Hernandez, Simon Calasanz, Dr. Apoorva Ranjan Sharma, Robin Heng, August Hatecke...thank you for taking the time out of your extremely busy schedule to read the manuscript and provide your valuable endorsement for book. It means a lot to me and I am deeply humbled!

To Mike Duplessis, Paula Vogliazzo, Drake Shergill, Xuan Wang, Mehdi Tahri, Alvin Lam, Carla Glasspool, Stephen Hegarty, Pat Joe, Kieran Callaghan, Isha Shah, Roxanna Gheorghiu...thank you all for volunteering to be a part of the Beta group representing four generations, five continents, and nine countries. Your diverse inputs, perspectives, insights and suggestions made this book significantly better.

It really took a whole *(global)* village to bring this project to fruition. To ABS-CBN Books team: Mark Yambot, Kristine Hernandez, Karen Odcenada, for publishing, printing, distributing and promoting the book in the Philippines; Happy Self Publishing Team: Jyotsna Ramachandran for keeping a close eye on the progress of the book and Sushmitha Naroor for project managing it from start to finish; Team Asia folks: Monette Hamlin and Bea Lim for helping organize and promote the book launch event; and a network of freelancers from around the world: Brock Swinson (US) for valuable insights and suggestions for the book, Phil Owens (Italy) for copy editing and proof reading, Fiaz Irfan (Indonesia) for the book cover design, Meet Patel (India) for website design, Musthafa Mohamed (India) for coding the website and bringing it to life, Matheus Jordann (Brazil) for designing the advocacy logo, and Yemi Adigun (Nigeria) for the book trailer. Because of all of your support, I was able to stay focused on researching, writing and editing. My sincere gratitude to each and every one of you.

To the Philippines – the beautiful country I have called home for the past 14 years! In many ways, this is a tribute to this memorable chapter of my life. As my family and I turn a page and start a new chapter in Singapore, I want to recognize our Filipino friends and colleagues for their kindness, warmth, and friendship over the years.

To the Higher Being…like in any creative pursuit, I was merely a channel and a medium for this book to flow through. I humbly offer this book back to the sacred place in the universe from where the inspiration, intuition, and ideas emerge.

INDEX

#
#maskchallenge, 118

$
$1 trillion market cap, 99

&
&Pizza, 118, 119

1
10,000 stories challenge, 164

2
2001 A Space Odyssey, 135
2054 Bible, 132
20th Century Fox, 129
21st Century, 21
24-carat gold, 96, 97, 98, 99

3
3M Corporation, 167

9
99designs, 59

A
A Game Plan for Life The Power of Mentoring, 107
Acres of Diamonds, 97
adapting, 18, 23, 33, 180
Afroz Shah, 84, 86, 240
agile, 19, 86, 122, 152, 172, 205, 206, 207, 250, 251
agility, 60, 87, 206, 207, 216
AHA, 192
AI, 15, 22, 31, 32, 33, 34, 35, 36, 37, 38, 39, 42, 43, 67, 69, 70, 71, 72, 73, 74, 76, 77, 78, 122, 135, 136, 142, 183, 184, 185, 187, 188, 189, 190, 215, 217, 234, 235, 239
Alabama, 28
Alaska, 17, 23, 217
alchemist, 22, 67, 95, 96, 97, 98, 99, 101, 107, 108, 145, 215
Alexa, 42, 131, 143, 188
algorithm, 37, 38, 71, 72, 73, 76
Alibaba, 59, 235
Amazon, 19, 35, 36, 47, 72, 87, 142, 171, 176, 181, 182, 183, 202, 205, 207, 209, 210, 219, 239, 240, 248, 251
Amazon Go stores, 36
Amazonians, 182
Amazons, 87, 184
America, 23, 55, 57, 58, 108, 238, 247
American Consulate in Mumbai, 57
American Dream, 57
America Online, 57
AND.CO, 55
Angel, 38
any-collar, 34
Apartheid, 82
Apple, 76, 98, 99, 135, 171, 176, 241
Apprente, 34
App store, 98

Arthur Fry, 167
artificial intelligence, 19, 30, 188, 239
astronomer, 126
AT&T, 182, 183, 248
AT&Ts, 184
Auke Creek, 17
Australia, 55
Austria, 28
author, 126, 132, 173, 208, 219, 221
automation, 33, 36, 183, 185, 187, 239
automobile, 28, 128
Avaamo, 37

B

Baby Ariel, 47
Baby Boomers, 43, 45, 62, 199, 200, 236
Bahama, 18
Bain and Company, 158
bedbugs, 23, 233
Berlin Marathon, 213
Bibliotheca Universalis, 41
Bill Gates, 126
biosynthesis, 81
Blackberry, 18, 19, 171
Black Friday, 153, 161, 246
Blockbuster, 170, 171
Bloomingdale, 203
blue-collar, 34
Bob Bowman, 114
Boeing 737 800, 195
Borders Books, 171
Böttger, 95, 96, 108, 241
Brad Sellers, 113
breast cancer, 38
Brookings Institution, 33
Buffer, 209
Bulls, 112, 113
Business Process Outsourcing company, 191

C

C-3PO, 69, 74
Calcutta, 153, 154, 165, 246
captain, 22, 67, 109, 110, 111, 116, 215

Captain Shults, 109, 110, 111, 114, 121, 123
Care Angel, 38
career, 22, 25, 31, 64, 78, 88, 105, 111, 116, 123, 135, 136, 183, 215
Carol Dweck, 103
cars, 28, 131, 159
Casetext, 37
catalyst, 22, 67, 81, 82, 85, 86, 87, 88, 89, 90, 93, 215
CDO, 149, 150
CEO, 19, 46, 86, 87, 103, 146, 147, 149, 155, 165, 177, 186, 209, 241, 249
CEOs, 21, 44
changing, 17, 18, 20, 23, 57, 73, 90, 126, 134, 147, 171, 186, 193, 200, 217
Chapel Hills, 81
Charli, 47, 48
Charli D'Amelio, 47
chatbots, 188
Chatbots, 36
Chelsea James, 181, 187
chess champion, 76
Chicago, 112, 118
Chicago Bulls, 112
Chief Digital Officer (CDO), 149
China, 35, 44, 156
chlorophyll, 81
Christina Karin, 118, 119
Christmas, 109, 111
CIO, 146, 147
Clara, 20, 21, 70, 130, 161, 221
Clarke, 135, 244
Cleveland Cavaliers, 112
Clifford Stoll, 126
CNN, 41, 110, 240, 243, 246
Cobb, 195, 196, 211, 249
Columbus, 108
comfort zone, 42, 90, 91, 92, 114
company, 19, 22, 25, 31, 34, 46, 47, 51, 57, 58, 63, 72, 87, 88, 89, 98, 99, 100, 101, 103, 104, 118, 119, 120, 122, 131, 137, 139, 142, 143, 144, 145, 146, 147, 148, 150, 151, 153, 154, 155, 157, 158, 159, 161, 162, 163, 164, 165, 168, 169, 171, 172, 173, 174, 175, 176, 177, 178,

179, 181, 182, 183, 184, 185, 186, 187, 191, 192, 196, 197, 201, 202, 203, 204, 205, 206, 207, 208, 209, 210, 211, 216
Computer Aided Detection (CAD), 38
computing power, 20, 30
Cone/Porter Novelli 2019 study, 156
connectivity, 20, 46, 48, 57
Conrad Gessner, 41
conscience, 39, 74
consumers, 19, 20, 32, 155, 156
Corporate Social Responsibility, 51, 216
Coursera, Udacity, 183
Covid19, 39, 116, 117, 119, 122
Covid19 crisis, 39
Craig Ehlo, 113
creativity, 40, 55, 71, 74, 169, 181, 188, 189
crowdfunding, 44
crowdsourcing, 44
CSR, 51
C-Suite, 150, 177
Cuba, 18
customers, 216
Customer Service industry, 36
CVS, 154, 246
CVS Pharmacy, 154

D

dad, 192, 193
Darryl Zanuck, 129
data, 19, 20, 30, 33, 37, 38, 41, 71, 72, 73, 152, 182, 187, 189, 209
David, 190, 192, 206, 207, 245, 249
David Beckham, 190
David Beckhams, 192
decade, 20, 22, 25, 31, 42, 46, 54, 58, 62, 86, 88, 97, 142, 144, 183, 187, 189, 200, 236, 238
Dell, 47, 236
digital camera, 19, 141
digital endocrine system, 70
digital generations, 19, 46, 49, 54, 62, 122, 135, 136, 142, 144, 198, 200
Digital Natives, 15, 25, 235

Digital revolution, 20
Discriminator, 71
disruption, 19, 29, 183, 184, 203, 204
Domino's, 142, 143, 144, 245
Domino's Pizza, 142, 143
dopamine, 70
drawn trolley, 28
Dr. Benjamin Hardy, 90
Dr. Eiji Nakatsu, 74
Dr. Hooman Samani, 69
Dr. Nakatsu, 75, 76
Dr. Richard Wolfenden, 81
Dr. Seuss, 81, 83
Dylan, 71
Dynamic Teen Company, 85
Dynamic Yield, 35

E

Eastman Kodak, 141, 245
eBay, 59, 193
Economist, 29
economy, 20, 29, 30, 62, 142, 155, 170, 200, 237
Edvard Munch, 72
Efren Peñaflorida, 85, 240
Ehlo, 113
Einstein, 17, 18, 23
Eliud Kipchoge, 213, 251
Elon Musk, 99, 241
empathy, 39, 70, 74, 208
employee handbook, 163
employees, 19, 22, 32, 47, 49, 63, 64, 86, 99, 103, 105, 117, 118, 119, 134, 139, 142, 144, 145, 146, 147, 148, 150, 151, 152, 155, 156, 157, 158, 160, 161, 163, 164, 168, 171, 177, 178, 181, 182, 183, 184, 185, 186, 187, 188, 189, 190, 191, 197, 198, 201, 202, 203, 204, 205, 207, 208, 209, 210, 216, 217, 247, 249, 251
endorphin, 70
engineering, 56, 72, 76, 78, 181, 183, 250
England, 29
entrepreneurial, 43, 44, 47, 62, 198, 201, 202
ESPN, 114, 242

evolution, 17, 233
evolve, 17, 18, 23, 233
evolving, 17, 18, 23, 43, 44, 46, 155, 156, 186, 233
expedition, 22, 139, 202, 203, 206, 211
extinction, 18, 104, 216, 217
Extinction, 15, 213, 217, 219, 251
extraordinary, 22, 67, 83, 84, 85, 215

F

Facebook, 43
Face ID, 31
face recognition, 35
farmworkers, 29
first industrial revolution, 29
flight 1380, 109, 114, 115, 123
Flippy, 35
Florida, 17, 18, 23, 50, 217, 233
FlyZoo hotel, 35, 36
forces, 20, 25, 142, 148, 179, 216
Ford, 27, 28, 128, 192, 203
Ford Motor Company, 128
Fortune, 19, 164, 198, 247
Fortune magazine, 19
fourth industrial revolution, 30
Fred Alan Wolf, 95, 96
freelance, 53, 58, 198, 237, 238
Freelance, 53, 237, 238
Freelancer, 58, 59
freelancers, 54, 55, 56, 58, 59, 60, 61, 62, 64, 122, 135, 136, 185, 187, 223, 238
Freelancers, 60, 61, 238
freelancing, 20, 55, 56, 58, 59, 62, 63, 64, 134, 238
From the Earth to the Moon, 136, 244
futureproof, 22, 78, 123, 145, 187, 215, 216
Future Ready, 183
futurist, 22, 67, 128, 131, 132, 137, 138, 216
futuristic, 31, 58

G

Gallup study, 157
GAN, 71
Gates, 126, 127, 129, 244
Gecko, 77
Gender inequality, 82
Generative Adversarial Network, 71
Generator, 71
Gen Xers, 43, 199
Gen Z, 43, 45, 46, 47, 48, 51, 62, 236, 237
Gen Zers, 47, 49, 51, 155, 192, 193, 217
Georgia Tech, 182, 183
Gessner, 41, 42
gig economy, 20, 62, 142, 237
Gillette razor, 175
Glassdoor, 47, 236
GM, 203
Gmail, 32, 125
GOAT — Greatest Of All Time, 169
gold, 95, 96, 97, 98, 99, 101, 105, 108, 145, 160, 215
Goliath, 206, 207
Goliaths, 206, 207
Google, 32, 38, 42, 44, 45, 47, 143, 174, 190, 192, 202, 205, 206, 207, 209, 235, 250
Google Books, 174
Google Earth, 174
Google Health, 38
Google Home, 143
Google Maps, 174
Google search, 32, 45
Green Bay Packers, 104
green lizards, 17, 18, 23, 217
Greta effect, 50
Greta Thunberg, 50
Grover Cleveland, 116
growth, 20, 43, 56, 58, 59, 99, 102, 108, 145, 213, 217, 237

H

half-naked fakir, 102
Hall of Famers, 104, 105
Handbook on the Knowledge Economy, 173

Hangzhou, China, 35
Healthcare industry, 38
heart, 39, 40, 50, 76, 106, 159, 213, 215, 222
hemoglobin, 81
Henry Ford, 27, 28, 128, 192
Herb Kelleher, 195, 196, 249
Hillary Clinton, 190
Hilton, 36
His Airness, 113
horse, 27, 28, 128, 138, 145, 149
horses, 27, 28, 29, 136
Hotmail, 125
humanoid, 31, 40, 188
humans, 29, 30, 34, 39, 42, 47, 69, 70, 71, 73, 76, 77, 100, 188, 241
humility, 21, 103
Hyundai, 131

I

IBM, 47, 126
India, 44, 56, 57, 58, 77, 98, 102, 104, 108, 192, 223, 238
Indiana Jones, 96
industrial revolution, 29, 30
industry, 28, 30, 34, 35, 36, 37, 38, 58, 59, 87, 122, 137, 142, 154, 171, 175, 176, 177, 197, 198, 203, 207, 216
ING, 206, 207, 250
Innosight, 19, 233
innovation, 22, 29, 45, 139, 168, 169, 171, 172, 173, 174, 175, 176, 177, 178, 180, 204, 205, 216, 248
Innovation, 15, 173, 178, 248
innovations, 28, 44, 180
innovative, 78, 172, 173, 174, 175, 178, 189, 191
internal combustion engine, 28
International Space Station, 100
international urban planning conference, 28
Internet, 42, 43, 46, 48, 57, 59, 62, 125, 126, 127, 201, 243, 244
intersection, 76, 77
intrapreneurs, 202
intuition, 40, 74, 189, 223
invention, 28, 41, 141, 168

iPad, 76, 135, 244
iPhone, 98, 176
iPod, 98
Ivanhoe, 53
IVR, 37

J

Jacob Sartorius, 47
James, 181, 182, 187, 234, 237, 244, 249
Janet, 191, 192
Janet Belarmino, 191
Janet Belarminos, 192
Japan Railway West, 74
JD Power, 164, 197
JD Power award for customer satisfaction, 164
Jeff Bezos, 87, 210, 240, 251
JetBlue, 159, 164, 165, 247
JFK, 97
Jimi Hendrix, 89
Johann Friedrich Böttger, 95, 241
John Maynard Keynes, 30
John Underkoffler, 132
John Wooden, 106
Jon Poteet, 117
Jules Verne, 136
Julius Hock, 28

K

Kantar Purpose 2020 study, 157
Kaptagat, Kenya, 214
Kareem Abdul Jabbar, 107
Kelleher, 195, 196, 198, 249
Kellogg, 159
Kenya, 57, 214
Kingfisher, 75, 76
King George V, 102
King of Poland, 95
King of Prussia, 95
Kipchoge, 213, 214, 215, 251
Kodak, 18, 19, 141, 142, 203, 244, 245
Kool-aid, 87
KPMG, 164, 247

L

Lady Gaga, 190
Lady Gagas, 192
LaGuardia airport, 110
Larry Nance, 113
law firms, 37
LawGeex, 37
LD, 186, 189, 193
learning, 22, 33, 34, 38, 39, 65, 72, 73, 78, 131, 139, 180, 183, 186, 187, 190, 204, 217
Learning and Development (LD), 186
Legal industry, 37
legal research, 37
Leonardo da Vinci, 78, 240
Let my people go surfing, 163
Liberal Arts, 76
LinkedIn, 137
Lombardi, 104, 105, 242
London, 27
Lovotics, 69

M

machine learning algorithm, 38, 73
Macy's, 203
Madeleine Albright, 141
Mahatma Gandhi, 98, 102
Malala Yousafzai, 50, 82, 86
mammograms, 38, 78, 235
mammography, 38
Management School, 55
Mandela, 82, 83, 84, 93
Manhattan, 27
manure, 27, 28
March For Our Lives, 50
Marines, 105
Mark Weiser, 31
Martha, 195, 196, 211, 249
Martha Cobb, 195, 211
Maslow, 213, 217
Maurten's Hydrogels, 214
mavericks, 87, 88
McDonald, 34, 235
McDonald's, 34, 235
McKinsey, 33, 54, 145, 150, 179, 183, 187, 234, 237, 245, 248, 249, 250, 251
McKinsey Global Institute, 54
McKinsey study, 145, 150, 179, 183, 187
Me Generation, 45, 236
Michael Jordan, 113, 114, 242
Michael Phelps, 88, 114, 242
Michigan Savings Bank, 128
microbes, 127
Microsoft, 47, 98, 103, 126, 127, 159, 177, 241, 244
Microsoft Co-founder, 127
Millennials, 43, 45, 46, 47, 51, 62, 155
Milton Friedman, 51
mini startups, 205, 207
Minority Report, 132, 244
Miso Robotics, 35
MIT, 132
Model, 100, 250
mom, 169, 171
Mona Lisa, 78
Monday morning blues, 199
morals, 73, 74
Moscow, 77
Most Valuable Player, 138
Mother Teresa, 153, 154, 246
Mount Everest, 191
Mozart, 188
Muhammad Ali, 99
Mumbai, 57, 84
Munch, 72, 239
musical.ly, 48

N

Nathaniel Meyers, 182, 187
National Taipei University, Taiwan, 69
natural language processing, 37
NCAA, 107
Neil Armstrong, 97
Nelson Mandela, 82
Netflix, 31, 170, 171, 200, 202, 205, 207, 209
Newspad, 135
Newsweek magazine, 126
New York City, 23, 27, 28, 217
New York Times, 51, 100, 237, 241, 244, 245

New York Times Magazine, 51
New Zealand, 55
NFL, 105
NHL, 138
Nikola Tesla, 136, 244
Nobel Peace Prize, 50
Nobel prize, 84
Nokia, 171
North American Airline Satisfaction Study, 197
Not missiles, 127

O

Olympic, 114
Olympic Gold Medals, 114
Olympics, 101
one-trick-ponies, 77, 78
one-trick-pony, 78
ordinary, 22, 67, 83, 84, 192, 215
organizational structure, 177, 203, 207
ornithology, 76
out-of-control flight (OCF), 115
Oxford University, 32
oxytocin, 70, 208, 211

P

Packers, 104, 105
Papa John's, 142
Parks, 82, 83, 84, 86, 93
Patagonia, 153, 163, 246, 247
Paul Krugman, 190
Paul Zak, 208
Perkbox, 61, 238
Personality Isn't Permanent, 90
Philippines, 57, 85, 191, 222, 223
Philosopher's stone, 95, 96
Picasso, 71
pink salmon, 17, 217
Pizza Hut, 142, 144, 245
playoff, 112
politically incorrect, 73
Porsche, 144
Porter Novelli/Cone, 49, 237, 246
Portland, Oregon, 117
Portrait of Edmond Belamy, 70
Post-It Note, 168, 248

Poteet, 117, 118
powered, 35, 36, 43, 69
prediction, 27, 30, 126
President John F. Kennedy, 97
printing press, 41, 42, 44
productivity, 29, 30, 158
Project Apollo, 97
prosperity, 29, 30
Psychology Today, 41
Purple Star, 193
purpose, 22, 49, 51, 120, 139, 153, 154, 155, 156, 157, 158, 159, 160, 161, 162, 163, 164, 165, 192, 216, 246, 247
purpose-driven, 49, 157, 158

R

radiologists, 38
Radisson Blu, 36
resumes, 72, 73, 113, 206
Richard Branson, 192
robot, 35, 36, 40, 69, 70, 77, 188, 235, 239
robotics, 33
robot "Pepper", 40
robots, 29, 31, 36, 133, 235, 239
Rolodex, 63
Rosa Parks, 82, 86
Rosetta Stone, 93
Ruelos, 117, 118
Rumi, 82
Russell Conwell, 97
ruthless prioritization, 121
Ryan Ruelos, 117

S

Salt Lake City, 196, 211, 249
Samsung, 171
Santa Monica, 132
Sasson, 141, 142
Satya Nadella, 103, 177, 241
Savannah, 90, 93, 221
Sci-fi novels, 31
Sears, 171, 203
second industrial revolution, 29
Secretary Albright, 142
Segregation, 82

Serena Williams, 88
serotonin, 70
Shakespeare, 41
Sheryl Sandberg, 121
Shine Distillery and Grill, 117
Shults, 109, 110, 111, 114, 121, 123, 243
Silicon Valley, 172
Silver Shooting Star, 193
Sir Arthur C Clarke, 135
Sir Walter Scott, 53
Sir William Preece, 128
Skynet, 31
smart machines, 20, 40
smartphone, 31, 32, 43, 48, 201
Smirnoff, 154, 246
Smirnoff Equalizer, 154
Snapchatting, 49
social media, 32, 43, 44, 48, 84, 200, 209, 219
Sophia, 188
South Africa, 164
Southwest, 109, 114, 195, 196, 197, 198, 242, 243, 249, 250
Southwest Airlines, 114, 195, 196, 243, 249, 250
Southwest flight 1380, 109
S&P 500, 19, 179
SpaceX, 100, 241
Spiderman, 75
Spielberg, 132
Spotify, 32, 154, 202, 205, 206, 207, 246, 250
Starbucks, 61, 62, 91
start-up, 172, 176, 205, 209
steam engine, 44
Stephen Covey, 173
Steve Jobs, 76, 98, 99, 176, 240, 241
Steven Sasson, 141
Steven Spielberg, 132
Stoll, 126, 127, 244
study, 32, 33, 47, 49, 54, 55, 76, 78, 81, 132, 133, 136, 145, 150, 156, 157, 179, 183, 187, 199, 208, 216, 237, 238, 240, 247, 249, 250

T

Taganskaya Square, 77, 79
Talks at Google, 190
Tammie Jo Shults, 109, 243
technology, 19, 20, 29, 30, 31, 35, 38, 42, 43, 44, 45, 46, 47, 57, 62, 73, 76, 112, 126, 133, 134, 135, 136, 141, 144, 145, 146, 174, 175, 183, 185, 187, 207, 216, 235, 236, 240
TED talk, 127
Terminator, 31
Tesla, 100, 136, 159, 241, 244
TGIF!, 199
Thanksgiving, 153
The British Post Office, 128
The Chief Engineer, 128
The Growth Mindset, 103
The Hotel of the Future, 35
The Internet? Bah!, 126
The Internet Tidal Wave, 126
The Lorax, 81
The scream, 72
The Times, 27
think tank summit, 132, 135
third industrial revolution, 29
Thucydides, 53, 55
Tickle Me Elmo, 125
Tiger Woods, 113
TikTok, 48, 49, 132
Timberland, 154, 246
Time magazine, 84, 85
Tim Ferris, 92
Tim Kastelle, 173, 248
Tom Brady, 113
Tony Robbins, 120
Toptal, 59
Toys R US, 18, 19
transportation, 27, 28, 136, 142
True North, 161
Trust Factor, 208
turbulence, 20, 111, 116, 122, 210
Twitch, 182

U

Uber, 56, 60, 131, 142, 174
UCLA basketball team, 106
U-Haul, 118, 119, 243

UK, 55, 61, 233, 238
University of Exeter, 55
University of North Carolina, 81
University of Notre Dame, 183
Upwork, 56, 58, 59, 238
US, 18, 19, 29, 33, 35, 37, 44, 50, 55, 56, 57, 58, 63, 114, 115, 116, 141, 154, 156, 157, 164, 169, 183, 197, 223, 248
US Navy, 114, 115

V

values, 51, 74, 93, 102, 119, 120, 157, 162, 163
Vegas, 163
Vince Lombardi, 104, 242
virtual nursing assistant, 38
Vision Mission Values, 119
VMV, 120
Vodka, 154

W

Walmart, 36, 63, 171
Walt Disney, 192
Washington DC, 50
Wayne Gretzky, 125, 138, 244
Waze, 77
WeWork, 62
white-collar, 34
Wi-Fi, 45
Wizard of Westwood, 107
womenswear designer, 118
Wooden, 106, 107
workers, 29, 33, 54, 55, 60, 62, 63, 64, 118, 126, 157, 183, 197, 199, 234, 238, 243
workforce, 22, 43, 44, 54, 56, 58, 62, 139, 145, 158, 183, 184, 185, 200, 217, 238, 248
work-from-home policy, 131

X

Xanax, 92
X-Rays, 78

Y

Yousafzai, 50, 82, 83, 84, 86, 93
YouTube, 44, 48, 131, 196

Z

Zak, 208, 251
Zappos, 159, 163, 247
Zara, 36

NOTES

Introduction

[1] Gilbert, Natasha. "Pink salmon evolve to migrate earlier in warmer waters." Nature News, July 11, 2012. https://www.nature.com/news/pink-salmon-evolve-to-migrate-earlier-in-warmer-waters-1.10993

[2] Science Connected. "Florida Lizards Evolving Rapidly." *Science Connected Magazine,* October 24, 2014. https://magazine.scienceconnected.org/2014/10/florida-lizards-evolving-rapidly/

[3] Anthony, Scott D., Viguerie, S. Patrick, Schwartz, Evan I., and Landeghem, John Van. "2018 Corporate Longevity Forecast: Creative Destruction in Accelerating." *Innosight*, February 2018. https://www.innosight.com/insight/creative-destruction/

[4] Resource library: Evo in the news. "Bed bugs bite back thanks to evolution." *Understanding Evolution*, September 2010. https://evolution.berkeley.edu/evolibrary/news/100901_bedbugs

Chapter 1 Artificial Intelligence

[1] Johnson, Ben. "The Great Horse Manure Crisis of 1894." *Historic UK*. https://www.historic-uk.com/HistoryUK/HistoryofBritain/Great-Horse-Manure-Crisis-of-1894/

[2] Kolbert, Elizabeth. "Hosed." *Books, The New Yorker*, November 16, 2009. https://www.newyorker.com/magazine/2009/11/16/hosed

[3] Hallman, Carly. "A Timeline of Car History." *Titlemax*. https://www.titlemax.com/articles/a-timeline-of-car-history/

[4] History.com Editors. "Industrial Revolution." *History*, October 29, 2009.
https://www.history.com/topics/industrial-revolution/industrial-revolution

[5] Richmond Vale. "Second Industrial Revolution: The Technological Revolution." *Richmond Vale Academy*, July 21, 2016. https://richmondvale.org/en/blog/second-industrial-revolution-the-technological-revolution

[6] Schwab, Klaus. "The Fourth Industrial Revolution: what it means, how to respond." *World Economic Forum*, January 14, 2016. https://www.weforum.org/agenda/2016/01/the-fourth-industrial-revolution-what-it-means-and-how-to-respond/

[7] Frey, Carl Benedikt and Osborne, Michael A. "The Future of Employment: How Susceptible are Jobs to Computerisation?" *Oxford Martin School*, September 27, 2013. https://www.oxfordmartin.ox.ac.uk/downloads/academic/The_Future_of_Employment.pdf

[8] Manyika, James, Lund, Susan, Chui, Michael, Bughin, Jacques, Woetzel, Jonathan, Batra, Parul, Ko, Ryan, and Sanghvi, Saurabh. "Jobs lost, jobs gained: What the future of work will mean for jobs, skills, and wages." *McKinsey & Company*, November 28, 2017. https://www.mckinsey.com/featured-insights/future-of-work/jobs-lost-jobs-gained-what-the-future-of-work-will-mean-for-jobs-skills-and-wages

[9] Muro, Mark, Whiton, Jacob, and Maxim, Robert. "What jobs are affected by AI? Better-paid, better-educated workers face the most exposure." *Brookings*, November 20, 2019. https://www.brookings.edu/research/what-jobs-are-affected-by-ai-better-paid-better-educated-workers-face-the-most-exposure/

[10] Barrett, Brian. "McDonald's Doubles Down on Tech with Voice AI Acquisition." *Wired*, September 10, 2019. https://www.wired.com/story/mcdonalds-acquires-apprente-voice-ai/

[11] https://misorobotics.com/flippy/

[12] Biron, Bethany. "Chinese e-commerce giant Alibaba has a hotel run almost entirely by robots that can serve food and fetch toiletries – take a look inside." *Business Insider*, October 22, 2019. https://www.businessinsider.com/alibaba-hotel-of-the-future-robots-ai-2019-10

[13] https://avaamo.ai/ai-platform/

[14] https://www.lawgeex.com

[15] https://casetext.com

[16] https://www.careangel.com

[17] Park, Alice. "Google's AI Bested Doctors in Detecting Breast Cancer in Mammograms." *Health, Artificial Intelligence, Time*, January 1, 2020 https://time.com/5754183/google-ai-mammograms-breast-cancer/

[18] Lim, Megumi, Chehui Peh, and Foster, Malcolm. "In Japan, robot-for-hire programmed to perform Buddhist funeral rites." *Reuters*, August 23, 2017. https://www.reuters.com/article/us-japan-robot-priest/in-japan-robot-for-hire-programed-to-perform-buddhist-funeral-rites-idUSKCN1B3133

[19] "Pepper" the robot has a new job." *CBS News*, August 24, 2017. https://www.cbsnews.com/news/pepper-the-robot-has-a-new-job/

Chapter 2 Digital Natives

[1] Bell, Vaughan. "Don't Touch That dial!" *Slate*, February 15, 2010. https://slate.com/technology/2010/02/a-history-of-media-technology-scares-from-the-printing-press-to-facebook.html

[2] Ryan Jenkins, *The Generation Z Guide: The Complete Manual to Understand, Recruit and Lead the Next Generation* (Atlanta, GA, USA: Ryan Jenkins LLC, 2019)

[3] Spitznagel, Eric. "Generation Z is bigger than millennials – and they're out to change the world." *Living, NY Post*, January 25, 2020. https://nypost.com/2020/01/25/generation-z-is-bigger-than-millennials-and-theyre-out-to-change-the-world/

[4] Cohn, D'Vera and Taylor, Paul. "Baby Boomers Approach 65 – Glumly." *Pew Research Center*, December 20, 2010. https://www.pewsocialtrends.org/2010/12/20/baby-boomers-approach-65-glumly/

[5] Jenkins, Ryan. "How Generation Z Uses Technology and Social Media." *Ryan-Jenkins*. https://blog.ryan-jenkins.com/how-generation-z-uses-technology-and-social-media

[6] Patrick, Neil. "The Baby Boomers were nicknamed the "Me Generation" due to their perceived narcissism." *The Vintage News*, September 5, 2016. https://www.thevintagenews.com/2016/09/05/priority-baby-boomers-nicknamed-generation-due-perceived-narcissism/

[7] Villas-Boas, Antonio. "'Red Dead Redemption 2' would have taken almost 48 hours to download a decade ago – here's how far internet speeds have come." *Business Insider*, November 6, 2019. https://www.businessinsider.com/internet-speeds-have-gotten-dramatically-faster-over-past-decade-2019-11

[8] Dell Technologies. "Gen Z is here. Are you ready?" *Dell Technologies*. https://www.delltechnologies.com/en-ph/perspectives/gen-z.htm

[9] Moore, Emily. "The Top 10 Employers Attracting Gen Z Workers." *Glassdoor*, February 20, 2019. https://www.glassdoor.com/blog/top-employers-gen-z/

[10] Ranzetta, Tim. "Question of the Day: What percent of high school students want to start their own business." *NGPF Next Gen Personal*

Finance, August 27, 2018. https://www.ngpf.org/blog/entrepreneurship/question-of-the-day-what-percent-of-high-school-students-want-to-start-their-own-business/

[11] News Provided by Porter Novelli/Cone. "90 Percent Of Gen Z Tired Of How Negative And Divided Our Country Is Around Important Issues, According to Research By Porter Novelli/Cone." Source Porter Novelli/Cone, *PR Newswire*, October 23, 2019. https://www.prnewswire.com/news-releases/90-percent-of-gen-z-tired-of-how-negative-and-divided-our-country-is-around-important-issues-according-to-research-by-porter-novellicone-300943452.html

[12] https://marchforourlives.com

[13] Friedman, Milton. "A Friedman doctrine—The Social Responsibility Of Business Is To Increase Its Profits." *The New York Times*, September 13, 1970. https://www.nytimes.com/1970/09/13/archives/a-friedman-doctrine-the-social-responsibility-of-business-is-to.html

Chapter 3 The Gig Economy

[1] Blackstock, J. "The Origin of the Word Freelance and Why it Should Make Us Happy." *Medium*, June 11, 2013 https://medium.com/@patterncapturer/the-origin-of-the-word-freelance-and-why-it-should-make-us-happy-84e46a206348

[2] Blackstock, J. "The Origin of the Word Freelance and Why it Should Make Us Happy." *Medium*, June 11, 2013 https://medium.com/@patterncapturer/the-origin-of-the-word-freelance-and-why-it-should-make-us-happy-84e46a206348

[3] Manyika, James, Lund, Susan, Bughin, Jacques, Robinson, Kelsey, Mischke, Jan, and Mahajan, Deepa. "Independent work: Choice, necessity, and the gig economy." *McKinsey & Company*, October 10, 2016. https://www.mckinsey.com/featured-insights/employment-and-growth/independent-work-choice-necessity-and-the-gig-economy

[4] The University of Sheffield Faculty of Social Sciences News. "Self-employed people happier and more engaged at work, study

finds." *The University Of Sheffield*, March 19, 2018. https://www.sheffield.ac.uk/social-sciences/news/self-employed-people-happier-and-more-engaged-work-study-finds

[5] https://www.and.co/slash-workers

[6] "Freelancing in America: 2019 Study Commissioned by Upwork and Freelancers union." *Upwork*, March 2019. https://www.upwork.com/press/2019/10/03/freelancing-in-america-2019/

[7] https://www.freelancer.com

[8] From Wikipedia, the free encyclopedia. "Upwork." *Wikipedia*. https://en.wikipedia.org/wiki/Upwork

[9] "Freelancing in America: 2017 Freelancers predicted to become the U.S. workforce majority within a decade, with nearly 50% of millennial workers already freelancing, annual "Freelancing in America" study finds." *Upwork*, October 17, 2017. https://www.upwork.com/press/2017/10/17/freelancing-in-america-2017/

[10] Rukshi. "The Up Demand For Freelancers (India 2019)." *Medium*, June 19, 2019. https://medium.com/@rukshanakk/the-up-demand-for-freelancers-india-2019-ed9b37b7185b

[11] "The 2020 UK workplace stress survey." *Perkbox*. https://www.perkbox.com/uk/resources/library/2020-workplace-stress-survey

[12] Monllos, Kristina. "Freelance freedom: Why working for yourself is becoming the new normal." *Digiday*, March 23, 2020. https://digiday.com/marketing/freelance-freedom-working-becoming-new-normal/

[13] Probasco, Jim. "The Rise of the Semi-Retired Life." *Investopedia*, November 25, 2019. https://www.investopedia.com/articles/retirement/102516/rise-semiretired-life.asp

Chapter 4 Future is AI: Be a Human

[1] The story originally aired on October 29, 2017 in an episode in Out in the Open radio program. "Can a robot love you back?" *CBC*, October 27, 2017. https://www.cbc.ca/radio/outintheopen/can-robots-be-human-1.4363742/can-a-robot-love-you-back-1.4364233

[2] Christies Features. "Is artificial intelligence set to become art's next medium?" *Christie's*. https://www.christies.com/features/A-collaboration-between-two-artists-one-human-one-a-machine-9332-1.aspx

[3] Michaud, Chris. "Munch's "The Scream" sells for record $120 million." *Reuters*, May 5, 2012. https://www.reuters.com/article/us-thescream-auction/munchs-the-scream-sells-for-record-120-million-idUSBRE84200M20120504

[4] From Wikipedia, the free encyclopedia. "The Scream." *Wikipedia*. https://en.wikipedia.org/wiki/The_Scream

[5] Dastin, Jeffrey. "Amazon scraps secret AI recruiting tool that showed bias against women." *Reuters*, October 10, 2018. https://www.reuters.com/article/us-amazon-com-jobs-automation-insight/amazon-scraps-secret-ai-recruiting-tool-that-showed-bias-against-women-idUSKCN1MK08G

[6] Dastin, Jeffrey. "Amazon scraps secret AI recruiting tool that showed bias against women." *Reuters*, October 10, 2018. https://www.reuters.com/article/us-amazon-com-jobs-automation-insight/amazon-scraps-secret-ai-recruiting-tool-that-showed-bias-against-women-idUSKCN1MK08G

[7] McKeag, Tom. "How one engineer's birdwatching made Japan's bullet train better." *The Biomimicry Column, GreenBiz*, October 19, 2012. https://www.greenbiz.com/article/how-one-engineers-birdwatching-made-japans-bullet-train-better

[8] AskNature Team. "Shinkansen Train." *Idea, Ask Nature*, September 19, 2017. https://asknature.org/idea/shinkansen-train/

[9] AskNature Team. "Shinkansen Train." *Idea, Ask Nature*, September 19, 2017. https://asknature.org/idea/shinkansen-train/

[10] Lehrer, Jonah. "Steve Jobs: "Technology Alone is not Enough." *News Desk, The New Yorker*, October 7, 2011. https://www.newyorker.com/news/news-desk/steve-jobs-technology-alone-is-not-enough

[11] Newcomb, Tim. "7 of the World's Wackiest Interchanges and Intersections." *Popular Mechanics*, June 15, 2018. https://www.popularmechanics.com/technology/infrastructure/g21239989/7-of-the-worlds-wackiest-interchanges-and-intersections/

[12] From Wikipedia, the free encyclopedia. "Leonardo da Vinci." *Wikipedia*. https://en.wikipedia.org/wiki/Leonardo_da_Vinci

Chapter 5 Future is Change: Be a Catalyst

[1] UNC School of Medicine Biochem News. "Without enzymes, biological reaction essential to life takes 2.3 billion years: UNC study." *UNC School of Medicine Biochemistry and Biophysics*, December 3, 2008. https://www.med.unc.edu/biochem/news/without-enzyme-biological-reaction-essential-to-life-takes-2-3-billion-years-unc-study/

[2] Toner, Kathleen. "CNN Hero Afroz Shah, He's doing the 'dirty work' to keep plastic out of the ocean." *CNN Heroes, Edition CNN*, October 17, 2019. https://edition.cnn.com/2019/10/17/world/cnn-heroes-afroz-shah-afroz-shah-foundation/index.html

[3] CNN Heroes. "CNN Hero Efren Peñaflorida, Pushcart educator named CNN Hero of the Year." *Edition CNN*, November 22, 2009. https://edition.cnn.com/2009/LIVING/11/16/cnnheroes.tribute.show/index.html

[4] Locke, Taylor. "Jeff Bezos looks for these 3 traits when hiring at Amazon." *Power Players, CNBC*, February 4, 2020. https://www.cnbc.

com/2020/02/04/jeff-bezos-looks-for-these-traits-when-hiring-at-amazon.html

Chapter 6 Future is People: Be an Alchemyst

[1] From Wikipedia, the free encyclopedia. "Johann Friedrich Böttger." *Wikipedia.* https://en.wikipedia.org/wiki/Johann_Friedrich_Böttger

[2] Yarow, Jay and Angelova, Kamelia. "CHART OF THE DAY: Apple's Incredible Run Under Steve Jobs." *Business Insider*, August 26, 2011. https://www.businessinsider.com/chart-of-the-day-apples-market-cap-during-steve-jobs-tenure-2011-8

[3] Nocera, Joe. "Costly Toys, or a New Era for Drivers?" *Talking Business, The New York Times*, July 19, 2008. https://www.nytimes.com/2008/07/19/business/19nocera.html

[4] Vengattil, Munsif and Bellon, Tina. "Musk defies skeptics, meets Tesla delivery goal; shares hit record." *Technology News, Reuters*, January 3, 2020. https://www.reuters.com/article/us-tesla-deliveries/musk-defies-skeptics-meets-tesla-delivery-goal-shares-hit-record-idUSKBN1Z21B5

[5] Morrison, Sara. "SpaceX finally sent humans to space. What happens next?" *Vox*, May 30, 2020. https://www.vox.com/recode/2020/5/30/21264937/spacex-nasa-elon-musk-dragon-capsule-human-launch

[6] Becque, Elien Blue. "Elon Musk Wants To Die On Mars." *Vanity Fair*, March 10, 2013. https://www.vanityfair.com/news/tech/2013/03/elon-musk-die-mars

[7] Gonsalves. Peter. "Half Naked Fakir, The Story of Gandhi's Personal Search for Sartorial Integrity." *Essay, part of the communication analysis on Gandhi's subversive use of clothing for liberation, M.K. Gandhi.* https://www.mkgandhi.org/articles/half-naked-fakir.html

[8] Bariso, Justin. "This Is the Book That Inspired Microsoft's Turnaround, According to CEO Satya Nadella." *Inc.*, November 26, 2018.

https://www.inc.com/justin-bariso/this-is-book-that-inspired-microsofts-turnaround-according-to-ceo-satya-nadella.html

[9] From Wikipedia, the free encyclopedia. "Vince Lombardi." *Wikipedia*. https://en.wikipedia.org/wiki/Vince_Lombardi

[10] Impelman, Craig. "Why You Should Always Give the Credit and Take the Blame." *Success*, May 2, 2018. https://www.success.com/why-you-should-always-give-the-credit-and-take-the-blame/

[11] Impelman, Craig. "Why You Should Always Give the Credit and Take the Blame." *Success*, May 2, 2018. https://www.success.com/why-you-should-always-give-the-credit-and-take-the-blame/

Chapter 7 Future is Turbulent: Be a Captain

[1] Schmidt, Samantha. "Nerves of Steel: She calmly landed the Southwest flight, just as you'd expect of a former fighter pilot." *Posted on Captainshults.com May 4, 2018, originally published in Washington Post*, April 18, 2018. https://www.captainshults.com/washington-post/

[2] From Wikipedia, the free encyclopedia. "The Shot." *Wikipedia*. https://en.wikipedia.org/wiki/The_Shot

[3] From Wikipedia, the free encyclopedia. "The Shot." *Wikipedia*. https://en.wikipedia.org/wiki/The_Shot

[4] MacMullan, Jackie. "The Michael Jordan I knew is about to be revealed to the world in 'The Last Dance'." *NBA Story, ESPN 5*, April 17, 2020. https://tv5.espn.com/nba/story/_/id/29041173/the-michael-jordan-knew-be-revealed-world

[5] O'Dowd, Sally. "Michael Phelps Visualized Success." *Medium*, November 20, 2018. https://medium.com/authority-magazine/michael-phelps-visualized-success-c4f5fc3b0b0a

[6] Shri SK Narvar. "Three Reasons to Think Before You Act." *SK Narvar Blog*, October 8, 2019. https://www.sknarvar.com/three-reasons-to-think-before-you-act/

⁷ Umoh, Ruth. "Southwest Airlines pilot who saved 149 people with emergency landing was one of the first women to fly fighter jets." *CNBC*, April 18, 2018. https://www.cnbc.com/2018/04/18/hero-southwest-airlines-pilot-was-one-of-first-women-to-fly-fa-18-hornet-in-navy.html

⁸ Koffman, Linda. "Business Unusual: A Distillery's In-House Hand Sanitizer Becomes a Local Hit." *Workest Powered by Zenefits*, June 9, 2020. https://www.zenefits.com/workest/business-unusual-a-distillerys-in-house-hand-sanitizer-becomes-a-local-hit/

⁹ Hofer, Elise. "Fashion Designers Join the Fight Against COVID-19 By Pivoting to Mask Production." *Marin Magazine*, April 2, 2020. https://marinmagazine.com/style/fashion/fashion-designers-join-the-fight-against-covid-19-by-pivoting-to-mask-production/

¹⁰ Haden, Jeff. "Expanded Sick Leave, $1 Per Hour Raise, Free Pizzas For Hospital Workers: One Company's Brilliant--and Expensive—Response to the Coronavirus Outbreak." *Inc.*, March 16, 2020. https://www.inc.com/jeff-haden/expanded-sick-leave-1-per-hour-raise-free-pizzas-for-hospital-workers-one-companys-brilliant-and-expensive-response-to-coronavirus-outbreak.html

¹¹ Guzman, Francisco and Ahmed, Saeed. "U-Haul offers 30-day storage free for college students who must suddenly move out." *Edition CNN*, March 13, 2020. https://edition.cnn.com/2020/03/13/us/uhaul-college-students-coronavirus-trnd/index.html

¹² Arnold, Kyle. " 'We couldn't see, we couldn't breathe': Tammie Jo Shults' book reveals how close Southwest 1380 came to total disaster." *Business, Airlines, The Dallas Morning News*, October 8, 2019. https://www.dallasnews.com/business/airlines/2019/10/08/couldnt-see-couldnt-breathe-tammie-jo-shults-book-reveals-close-southwest-1380-came-total-disaster/

Chapter 8 Future is Unknown: Be a Futurist

¹ Tech Musings. "The rather petite Internet of 1995." *Solarwinds Pingdom*, March 31, 2011. https://www.pingdom.com/blog/internet-1995/

[2] Stoll, Clifford. "Why the Web Won't Be Nirvana." *Tech & Science, Newsweek,* February 26, 1995. https://www.newsweek.com/clifford-stoll-why-web-wont-be-nirvana-185306

[3] Wired Staff. "May 26, 1995: Gates, Microsoft Jump om 'Internet Tidal Wave'." *Wired,* May 26, 2010. https://www.wired.com/2010/05/0526bill-gates-internet-memo/

[4] "The next outbreak? We're not ready." *Talks, TED,* March 2015. https://www.ted.com/talks/bill_gates_the_next_outbreak_we_re_not_ready?language=en

[5] From Wikipedia, the free encyclopedia. "Technologies in Minority Report." *Wikipedia.* https://en.wikipedia.org/wiki/Technologies_in_Minority_Report

[6] Rothkerch, Ian. "Will the future really look like "Minority Report"?" *Salon,* July 10, 2002. https://www.salon.com/2002/07/10/underkoffler_belker/

[7] Popova, Maria. "Arthur C. Clarke Predicts the iPad in 1968." *Brain Pickings,* March 15, 2012. https://www.brainpickings.org/2012/03/15/arthur-c-clarke-predicts-the-ipad-in-1968/

[8] Lim, Andrew. "Nikola Tesla predicted mobile phones in 1909." *Mobile Article, Recombu,* May 3, 2010. https://recombu.com/mobile/article/nikola-tesla-predicted-mobile-phones-in-1909_m11683-html

[9] From Wikipedia, the free encyclopedia. "From the Earth to the Moon." *Wikipedia.* https://en.wikipedia.org/wiki/From_the_Earth_to_the_Moon

[10] From Wikipedia, the free encyclopedia. "Wayne Gretzky." *Wikipedia.* https://en.wikipedia.org/wiki/Wayne_Gretzky

Chapter 9 Future is Digital: Transform Business

[1] Estrin, James. "Kodak's First Digital Moment." *Lens Blogs, The New York Times,* August 12, 2015.

https://lens.blogs.nytimes.com/2015/08/12/kodaks-first-digital-moment/

² Dang, Laura. "Why the Man Who Invented the Digital Camera in 1975 Was Forced to Keep it Hidden." *Business, NextShark*, August 18, 2015. https://nextshark.com/steven-sasson-kodak-digital-camera/

³ De la Merced, Michael J. "Eastman Kodak Files for Bankruptcy." *Legal/Regulatory Restructuring & Bankruptcy, Dealbook The New York Times*, January 19, 2012. https://dealbook.nytimes.com/2012/01/19/eastman-kodak-files-for-bankruptcy/

⁴ Associated Press. "Domino's old pizza's crust tasted like cardboard – try the new one." *Pizzaturnaround.com, Business, The Star*, January 12, 2010. https://www.thestar.com.my/business/business-news/2010/01/12/dominos-old-pizzas-crust-tasted-like-cardboard--try-the-new-one

⁵ "Domino's does digital ordering 15 ways on Super Bowl Sunday." *News, Pizza Marketplace*, February 2, 2018. https://www.pizzamarketplace.com/news/dominos-does-digital-ordering-15-ways-on-super-bowl-sunday/

⁶ Reid, David. "Domino's delivers world's first ever pizza by drone." *Tech Transformers CNBC*, November 16, 2016. https://www.cnbc.com/2016/11/16/dominos-has-delivered-the-worlds-first-ever-pizza-by-drone-to-a-new-zealand-couple.html

⁷ Edison. "Domino's takes 50% of pizza delivery market, leading Pizza Hut (29%) and Papa Johns (21%)." *Edison Discovers, Medium*, March 25, 2020. https://medium.com/edison-discovers/dominos-takes-50-of-pizza-delivery-market-leading-pizza-hut-29-and-papa-johns-21-6f8c11ef03a3

⁸ McKinsey & Company. "Unlocking success in digital transformation." *McKinsey & Company*, 2018. https://www.mckinsey.com/~/media/McKinsey/Business%20Functions/Organization/Our%20Insights/Unlocking%20success%20in%20digital%20transformations/Unlocking-success-in-digital-transformations.ashx

Chapter 10 Future is Meaningful: Instill Purpose

[1] Kavilanz, Parija. "Patagonia will donate 100% of its Black Friday sales." *Holiday Shopping CNN Money*, November 21, 2016. https://money.cnn.com/2016/11/21/news/patagonia-black-friday/index.html

[2] Glover, Erika. "Live Like Mother Teresa: Finding your own Calcutta." *Franciscan Media*, March 13, 2018. https://blog.franciscanmedia.org/franciscan-spirit/live-like-mother-teresa-finding-your-own-calcutta

[3] News Provided by Smirnoff. "SmirnoffTM and Spotify Debut New Experience Enabling You To Uncover Your Listening Habits To Promote Phenomenal Women." *PR Newswire*, March 2, 2018. https://www.prnewswire.com/news-releases/smirnoff-and-spotify-debut-new-experience-enabling-you-to-uncover-your-listening-habits-to-promote-phenomenal-women-300607349.html

[4] Henry, Zoë. "This Business Move Cost CVS $2 Billion (but It Was the Smartest Decision It Could Have Made)." *Inc.*, May 10, 2016. https://www.inc.com/zoe-henry/cvs-lost-2-billion-socially-conscious-business-move.html

[5] Peters, Adele. "Timberland is planting 50 million trees." *World Changing Ideas, Fast Company*, September 5, 2019. https://www.fastcompany.com/90399302/timberland-is-planting-50-million-trees

[6] Barton, Rachel, Ishikawa, Masataka, and Quiring, Kevin, Accenture Strategy. "To Affinity and Beyond From Me to We, The Rise of the Purpose-Led Brand." *Accenture*, 2018. https://www.accenture.com/_acnmedia/Thought-Leadership-Assets/PDF/Accenture-CompetitiveAgility-GCPR-POV.pdf

[7] News Provided by Porter Novelli. "Purpose Messages Evoke Greater Attention, Arousal And Emotion, According To First-Of-Its-Kind Biometrics Research By Porter Novelli/Cone." *PR Newswire*, May 29, 2019. https://www.prnewswire.com/news-releases/purpose-messages-evoke-greater-attention-arousal-and-emotion-according-to-first-of-its-kind-biometrics-research-by-porter-novellicone-300857801.html

[8] Aziz, Afdhel. "The Power Of Purpose: Kantar Purpose 2020 Study Shows How Purposeful Brands Grow Twice As Fast As Their Competition." *Forbes*, November 11, 2019. https://www.forbes.com/sites/afdhelaziz/2019/11/11/the-power-of-purpose-kantar-purpose-2020-study-shows-how-purposeful-brands-grow-twice-as-fast-as-their-competition/#4b727eff4236

[9] Harter, Jim. "Employee Engagement on the Rise in the U.S." *Economy News, Gallup*, August 26, 2018. https://news.gallup.com/poll/241649/employee-engagement-rise.aspx

[10] Garton, Eric, and Mankins, Michael. "Engaging Your Employees is Good, but Don't Stop There." *HBR.org, Bain & Company*, December 9, 2015. https://www.bain.com/insights/engaging-your-employees-is-good-but-dont-stop-there-hbr/

[11] Inc. Editorial, Inc. Staff. "24 Strange Questions You Might Hear During A Zappos Job Interview." *Inc.*, May 14, 2014. https://www.inc.com/jillian-donfo/strange-zappos-interview-questions.html

[12] Chouinard, Yvon. "Introducing a New Edition of Yvon Chouinard's "Let My People Go Surfing"." *Culture, Surfing, Patagonia*. https://www.patagonia.com/stories/let-my-people-go-surfing/story-30910.html

[13] Pfau, Bruce N. "How an Accounting Firm Convinced Its Employees They Could Change the World." *Employee Retention, Harvard Business Review*, October 6, 2015. https://hbr.org/2015/10/how-an-accounting-firm-convinced-its-employees-they-could-change-the-world

[14] News Provided by KPMG LLP. "KPMG Leads Big Four On Fortune's List Of 100 Best Companies To Work For." *PR Newswire*, March 5, 2015. https://www.prnewswire.com/news-releases/kpmg-leads-big-four-on-fortunes-list-of-100-best-companies-to-work-for-300046046.html

[15] Businesswire.com. "JetBlue Awarded Top Customer Satisfaction Honor Among Low Cost Carriers by J.D. Power in the 2019 North America Airline." *Business, Bloomberg*, May 29, 2019. https://www.bloomberg.com/press-releases/2019-05-29/jetblue-awarded-top-

customer-satisfaction-honor-among-low-cost-carriers-by-j-d-power-in-the-2019-north-america-airline

Chapter 11 Future is Boundless: Unleash Innovation

[1] Bellis, Mary. "Invention of the Post-It Note." *Humanities History & Culture ThoughtCo*, October 16, 2019. https://www.thoughtco.com/history-of-post-it-note-1992326

[2] Kastelle, Tim. "The Problem of Defining Innovation." *Tim Kastelle*, August 23, 2010. http://timkastelle.org/blog/2010/08/an-innovation-definition/

[3] Desmet, Driek, Duncan, Ewan, Scanian, Jay, and Singer, Marc. "Six building blocks for creating a high-performing digital enterprise." *McKinsey & Company*, September 1, 2015. https://www.mckinsey.com/business-functions/organization/our-insights/six-building-blocks-for-creating-a-high-performing-digital-enterprise

Chapter 12 Future is New: Inspire Learning

[1] Coyle, Meg. "Skills today for tomorrow's jobs." *Working at Amazon, About Amazon*, July 11, 2019. https://blog.aboutamazon.com/working-at-amazon/skills-today-for-tomorrows-jobs

[2] Caminiti, Susan. "AT&T's $1 billion gambit: Retraining nearly half its workforce for jobs of the future." *At Work, CNBC*, March 13, 2018. https://www.cnbc.com/2018/03/13/atts-1-billion-gambit-retraining-nearly-half-its-workforce.html

[3] Cullen, Terri. "Amazon plans to spend $700 million to retrain a third of its US workforce in new skills." *Tech, CNBC*, July 11, 2019. https://www.cnbc.com/2019/07/11/amazon-plans-to-spend-700-million-to-retrain-a-third-of-its-workforce-in-new-skills-wsj.html

[4] Caminiti, Susan. "AT&T's $1 billion gambit: Retraining nearly half its workforce for jobs of the future." *At Work, CNBC*, March 13, 2018. https://www.cnbc.com/2018/03/13/atts-1-billion-gambit-retraining-nearly-half-its-workforce.html

⁵ Manyika, James, Lund, Susan, Chui, Michael, Bughin, Jacques, Woetzel, Jonathan, Batra, Parul, Ko, Ryan, and Sanghvi, Saurabh. "Jobs lost, jobs gained: What the future of work will mean for jobs, skills, and wages." *McKinsey & Company*, November 28, 2017. https://www.mckinsey.com/featured-insights/future-of-work/jobs-lost-jobs-gained-what-the-future-of-work-will-mean-for-jobs-skills-and-wages

⁶ https://talksat.withgoogle.com

⁷ Johnson, Sarah. "Ready for Generation Z in the workplace?" *The Business Times*, May 8, 2019. https://thebusinesstimes.com/ready-for-generation-z-in-the-workplace/

Chapter 13 Future is Fun: Enjoy Expedition

¹ Cobb, Martha 'Marty'. Southwest Airlines flight to Salt Lake City, USA. "To activate the flow of oxygen simply insert 75 cents for the first minute.", *Speakola*. April 14, 2014. https://speakola.com/corp/marty-cobb-safety-announcment-2014

² Koenig, David AP Airlines Writer. "Herb Kelleher, co-founder of Southwest Airlines, dies at 87." *ABC News*, January 4, 2019. https://abcnews.go.com/Business/wireStory/herb-kelleher-founder-southwest-airlines-dies-87-60150011

³ Hoopfer, Evan Staff Writer, Dallas Business Journal. "Southwest Airlines CEO discusses 47-year profitability streak, HQ employees working from home and more." *Transportation, Houston Business Journals*, August 15, 2020. https://www.bizjournals.com/houston/news/2020/08/15/southwest-47-years-profitable-work-from-home.html

⁴ J.D. Power Press Release. "Importance of Trust, Transparency to Airline Satisfaction Grows as Industry Confronts Pandemic Fears, J.D. Power Finds." *J.D. Power*, May 27, 2020. https://www.jdpower.com/business/press-releases/2020-north-america-airline-satisfaction-study

[5] Robertson, Kristin. "Southwest Airlines Reveals 5 Culture Lessons." *Culture University Blog, Human Synergistics International*, May 29, 2018. https://www.humansynergistics.com/blog/culture-university/details/culture-university/2018/05/29/southwest-airlines-reveals-5-culture-lessons

[6] News Provided by Southwest Airlines Co. "Southwest Airlines Ranks No. 11 Among FORTUNE's World's Most Admired Companies." *Southwest Airlines Co., PR Newswire*, January 21, 2020. https://www.prnewswire.com/news-releases/southwest-airlines-ranks-no-11-among-fortunes-worlds-most-admired-companies-300990610.html

[7] Mautz, Scott. "New Study Shows a Surprising 81 Percent Feel 'Sunday Night Dread' About Work. (Here's What to Do)." *Inc.*, June 2, 2019. https://www.inc.com/scott-mautz/new-study-shows-a-surprising-81-percent-feel-sunday-night-dread-about-work-heres-what-to-do.html

[8] Ruderman, Zoe. "Make Monday Mornings Less Depressing." *Cosmopolitan*, July 29, 2011. https://www.cosmopolitan.com/health-fitness/advice/a3632/make-monday-mornings-less-depressing/

[9] Ageling, Willem-Jan. "Spotify Engineering Culture (Spotify Model) – an introduction Scaling Scrum, part 4." *Medium*, March 3, 2019. https://medium.com/serious-scrum/spotify-engineering-culture-spotify-model-an-introduction-500837f04010

[10] "Getting Hired at Spotify." *PathMatch*, August 22, 2020. https://www.pathmatch.com/blog/getting-hired-at-spotify

[11] Zetlin, Minda. "Google Automatically Rejects Most Resumes for Common Mistakes You've Probably Made Too." *Inc.*, April 9, 2018. https://www.inc.com/minda-zetlin/google-resume-mistakes-laszlo-bock-job-hiring-employment.html

[12] McKinsey Quarterly, Interview as conducted by Deepak Mahadevan, a partner in McKinsey's Brussels Office. "ING's agile transformation" *Peter Jacobs chief information officer of ING Netherlands, Bart Schlatmann, who left ING in January 2017 after 22 years with the group, is the former chief operating officer of ING*

Netherlands, Interview conducted in October 2016, *McKinsey & Company*, January 10, 2017. https://www.mckinsey.com/industries/financial-services/our-insights/ings-agile-transformation

[13] Vitasek, Kate. "Paul J. Zak: Doing the Math on Trust", *Future of Sourcing*, March 28, 2017. https://futureofsourcing.com/node/671

[14] https://www.slideshare.net/reed2001/culture-1798664

[15] https://buffer.com/about

[16] Umoh, Ruth. "Jeff Bezos to Amazon employees: If your boss says no, ask your boss' boss." *Leadership, CNBC*, September 27, 2018. https://www.cnbc.com/2018/09/26/amazon-ceo-jeff-bezos-if-your-boss-says-no-go-ask-someone-else.html

The Future: Growth or Extinction

[1] From Wikipedia, the free encyclopedia. "Eliud Kipchoge." *Wikipedia*. https://en.m.wikipedia.org/wiki/Eliud_Kipchoge

[2] "How Eliud Kipchoge Prepares for a Marathon: Part 1." *Believe in The Run*, October 7, 2019.
https://www.believeintherun.com/2019/10/07/how-eliud-kipchoge-prepares-for-a-marathon-part-1/

[3] "How Eliud Kipchoge Prepares for a Marathon: Part 2." *Believe in the Run*, October 8, 2019.
https://www.believeintherun.com/2019/10/08/how-eliud-kipchoge-prepares-for-a-marathon-part-2/

[4] Huber, Martin Fritz. "Wisdom from the World's Best Marathoner." *In Stride, Outside Online*, February 9, 2018.
https://www.outsideonline.com/2280201/wisdom-worlds-best-marathoner

[5] Agence France-Presse. "Kenyan Marathon Master Eliud Kipchoge Smashes World Record." *NDTV Sports*, September 16, 2018. https://sports.ndtv.com/othersports/kenyan-marathon-master-eliud-kipchoge-smashes-world-record-1917361

www.ingramcontent.com/pod-product-compliance
Lightning Source LLC
Chambersburg PA
CBHW060827220526
45466CB00003B/1000